This important new book addresses problems of empiricism within a pragmatic, decision theoretic framework. Skyrms applies this point of view to the analysis of chance, the theory of subjunctive conditionals, and the theory of rational decision itself.

Statements of chance play a significant role in statistical reasoning, but Skyrms argues that the analysis of chance via ergodic theory shows them to be pragmatically eliminable. He extends this central analysis of chance to other areas, giving subjunctive conditionals a Bayesian analysis involving conditional chance and reducing degrees of belief about subjunctive conditionals to degrees of belief about more ordinary propositions. According to Skyrms, decision theory itself is affected by causal and counterfactual considerations, but the concerns of "causal decision theory" are accommodated by taking expected value as an (unconditional) epistemic expectation of a (conditional) chance expectation. Skyrms views this decision theory as resting on standard convergence theorems rather than on any extravagant metaphysics of causation or possible worlds, for it too falls under the pragmatic reduction of chance.

This pragmatic version of empiricism illuminates and legitimizes concepts that other versions of empiricism render suspect. For this reason, it promises a more adequate framework for the analysis of science and should be of great interest to philosophers and social scientists concerned with epistemology and subjective probability.

D0992099

PRAGMATICS AND EMPIRICISM

BRIAN SKYRMS

PRAGMATICS AND EMPIRICISM

YALE UNIVERSITY PRESS
New Haven and London

91-346

Designed by Nancy Ovedovitz and set in Linotron Melior type by
Graphic Composition, Inc., Athens, Georgia. Printed in the United
States of America by BookCrafters, Inc., Chelsea, Michigan.

Library of Congress Cataloging in Publication Data
Skyrms, Brian.
    Pragmatics and empiricism.
    Includes bibliographical references and index.
    1. Empiricism.   2. Probabilities.   3. Chance.
4. Pragmatics.   I. Title.
B816.S59 1984   146'.44   84-5064
ISBN 0-300-03174-2 (alk. paper)

The paper in this book meets the guidelines for permanence and
durability of the Committee on Production Guidelines for Book
Longevity of the Council on Library Resources.

10   9   8   7   6   5   4   3   2   1

For Pauline and Michael

Contents

Preface

At one level the theme of this book is, as stated in chapter 1, that empiricism becomes a much more acceptable and illuminating doctrine when restated within a thoroughly pragmatic framework. That pragmatic framework is taken to involve heavily the theory of personal probability, whose foundations are discussed in chapter 2. That chapter contains an elementary and transparent presentation of Dutch book theorems for personal probability (including Dutch book arguments for conditionalization and for countable additivity). It also contains a discussion of the status of representation theorems for personal probability. At another level the book is about the interaction of two conceptions of probability—chance and degree of belief—and how generalizations of de Finetti's theorem show how degrees of belief act *as if* they were degrees of belief about chance, whether or not we really believe in the reality of chances. These generalizations of de Finetti's theorem and the light they throw on our conception of chance, and on induction in general, are discussed in chapter 3. Chapter 4 analyzes the interaction of chance and degree of belief in rational decision and shows how it is possible to subscribe to causal decision theory without really believing in chance or causal necessity. Chapter 5 generalizes some of the ideas in chapter 4 to give a general Bayesian theory of subjunctive conditionals which has the theories of Adams and Stalnaker as special cases. Chapter 6 takes an overview of the pragmatic variety of empiricism developed in the previous chapters, which is found to be less Procrustean and more discriminating than old-fashioned positivistic views.

Parts of this book make payments on intellectual promissory notes issued in my *Causal Necessity*. There it was argued that the representation of degrees of belief as the expectation of chance should be guided by considerations of *resiliency*. The chance distributions of the representation were to be resilient, that is, invariant under conditioning, with respect to some set of possible further specifications of the experimental setup. Questions remained as to how to choose the appropriate set over which resiliency is to be taken. In chapter 3, I show how the theory of measure-preserving transformations provides some substantive machinery for answering these questions. Metric indecomposability *is* resiliency. The ergodic decomposition theorem shows how an invariant subjective probability can be represented as a mixture of resilient objective probabilities.

In *Causal Necessity* I introduced very briefly the leading ideas of a Bayesian version of causal decision theory and of a Bayesian theory of subjunctive conditionals. In chapters 4 and 5 of this book, these ideas are developed in greater detail and are related to the viewpoint of chapter 3.

Chapters 1 and 6 give some idea of the general philosophical motivation for the kind of pragmatic analysis that I have been pursuing both in *Causal Necessity* and in the inner chapters of this book.

The generalizations of de Finetti's theorem in chapter 3 constitute the technical foundation for much of the rest of the work. They stand behind the formulation and justification of "causal" decision theory without recourse to causes of chapter 4 and the Bayesian theory of subjunctive conditionals of chapter 5. Some readers will find too little technical detail in chapter 3; some philosophers who do not specialize in the area may find too much. For the former, there are ample references to the literature. The latter can skip over technical detail, perhaps beginning by reading the first and last sections of the chapter, and then working inward as far as seems profitable. (The next-to-last section, "Invariance Resiliency and Ergodicity," makes the connection with *Causal Necessity*.) In chapters 4 and 5 as well it should be possible to skip over some technical details and still come away with a reasonable idea of the theories being proposed.

I am indebted to many friends and colleagues for discussion of the issues treated in this book, including Ernest Adams, Brad Armendt, Ellery Eells, Brian Ellis, Bill Harper, Richard Jeffrey, David Lewis, Terry Parsons, Bob Stalnaker, and Peter Woodruff. Use of the word processor at the Philosophy Department of the University of California at Irvine, together with careful proofreading by my wife, made it possible for a wildly inaccurate typist to produce a manuscript with minimal pain. Thanks to Maureen MacGrogan, Charlotte Dihoff, and Gladys Topkis of Yale University Press for seeing the manuscript into print.

1 Pragmatics and Empiricism

The fundamental tenet of modern empiricism is the view that all non-analytic knowledge is based on experience.

Carl G. Hempel
"The Empiricist Criterion of Meaning"

I had said that the problems of philosophy or of the philosophy of science are merely syntactical problems; I should have said in a more theoretical way that these are metatheoretical problems. . . . Later we saw that the realm of philosophy must also include semantics and pragmatics. . . .

Rudolf Carnap
"Intellectual Autobiography"

One of the characteristic features of logical empiricism, and one of the sources of its intellectual richness, was the inter-action between epistemology and the philosophy of language *via* the principle of empiricism. Language—and, since philosophical analysis was thought of as analysis of the relevant language, philosophical analysis in general—was put to the epistemological test. On the other hand, the conception of the principle of empiricism itself was influenced by contemporary theories of language. In this chapter, I will discuss this interaction and argue that many of the difficulties with the principle of empiricism were difficulties in for-

1

mulation due to an excessively restrictive philosophy of language.

SYNTAX

In the early years of the Vienna Circle, philosophy of language was focused on syntax. Indeed, one influential view was that semantics was a form of meaningless metaphysics. For some of the flavor of this, here are a few passages from Neurath's "Sociology and Physicalism" (1931):[1]

> Nor may language as a whole be set up against "experience as a whole", "the world", or "the given". Thus every statement of the kind: "The very possibility of science depends upon the fact of order in the universe" is meaningless. Such statements cannot be salvaged as "elucidations" to which a somewhat less strict criterion applies. There is little difference between such an attempt and metaphysics in a conventional sense.
>
> It is always science as a system of statements which is at issue. *Statements are compared with statements*, not with "experiences", "the world", or anything else. All these meaningless *duplications* belong to a more or less refined metaphysics and are, for that reason, to be rejected.

In *The Logical Syntax of Language* (1936),[2] Carnap maintained that the problems of philosophy are syntactical problems. In his foreword he italicized these theses: "Philosophy is to be replaced by the logic of science . . ." and ". . . the logic of science is nothing other than the logical syntax of the language of science."

If from our present point of view this concentration on syntax appears to be a debilitating fixation, we should remember that Carnap and Neurath were, in fact, rebelling against an even more restrictive doctrine. In his *Tractatus Logico-Philosophicus* Wittgenstein maintained that *all* metalinguistic statements, including syntactical ones, were meaningless. For Wittgenstein, the meaningful sentences consisted only in atomic sentences about the world, and truth functions thereof. He thought that this ruled out even syntactical metalinguistic statements. Neurath and Carnap disagreed. As Carnap recollects in his intellectual autobiography:[3]

> Neurath emphasized from the beginning that language events are events *within* the world, not something that refers to the world from outside. Spoken language consists of sound waves; written language consists of marks of ink on paper. Neurath emphasized these facts in order to reject the view that there is something "higher", something mysterious, "spiritual", in language, a view which was prominent in German philosophy. I agreed with him, but pointed out that only the structural pattern, not the physical properties of the ink marks, was relevant to the function of language. Thus, it is possible to construct a theory about language, namely the geometry of the written pattern. This idea led later to what I called the "logical syntax" of language.

Carnap and Neurath thus came to the conclusion that it was possible to have a scientific theory of syntax.

Carnap and Neurath had shining examples to hold up in their argument for the fruitful study of syntax. There was David Hilbert's *Grundlagen der Geometrie* (1899). In this virtuoso exercise in the axiomatic method, Hilbert emphasized that it was of central importance to the enterprise that the intuitive meanings of the geometrical terms involved were not to enter into the proofs. Proof was to be syntactical, depending only on the axioms and rules of inference. This method revealed how less rigorous treatments of geometry had relied on assumptions hidden by reliance on geometrical diagrams and intuition.

Then there was Hilbert's program for the foundations of mathematics. Hilbert wanted to establish by finitary means that the whole of mathematics is a conservative extension of finitary mathematics. For this it is necessary[4] to prove the consistency of mathematics by finitary means. Herman Weyl in his death notice of Hilbert (1944)[5] describes the program as follows:

> Hilbert agrees with Brower that the great majority of mathematical propositions are not "real" ones conveying a definite

meaning in the light of evidence. But he insists that the non-real, the "ideal" propositions, are indispensable to give our mathematical system "completeness". Thus he parries Brower who had asked us to give up what is meaningless, by relinquishing the pretension to meaning altogether, and what he tries to establish is not truth of the individual mathematical proposition, but *consistency* of the system. The game of deduction, he maintains, will never lead to the formula $0 \neq 0$.

This is a project even more thoroughly syntactical than that of the foundations of geometry, for, as Weyl points out:

> Whereas in his *Grundlagen der Geometrie* the meaning of the geometrical terms has become irrelevant, but the meaning of the logical terms . . . has still to be understood, now every trace of meaning has been obliterated.

When Hilbert's program for the foundations of mathematics was shown to be impossible by Gödel, it was by syntactical methods. Indeed, Carnap tells us in his intellectual autobiography that conversations with Gödel in 1930 about the arithmetization of syntax were instrumental in starting the train of thought that led to *The Logical Syntax of Language* in 1934.

So in the beginning logical positivists concentrated on syntax for both positive and negative reasons: the example of recent work by great mathematicians; and an ultra-fastidious attitude toward "metaphysics." This early syntactical set influenced the formulation of problems and the tentative solutions advanced by the empiricists long after Tarski convinced Carnap of the legitimacy of semantics. How can one have a syntactical theory of science? Everything must be done in terms of derivability and (syntactic) definability. Confirmation must be explained in terms of the deducibility of certain epistemically privileged sentences—the "protocol" sentences—from other sentences of the theory, scientific explanation as the deduction of sentences to be explained from suitable explaining sentences, and so forth. In short, we get the kind of hypothetico-deductive account which dominated philosophy of science for so long, and which eventually began to break up as a result of its internal problems.

The concentration on syntax, which in part sprang from the principle of empiricism, in turn influenced attempts to formulate the principle precisely. Thus, emphasis was put on *verifiability*, this being interpreted as *derivability* from a class of observation statements; or *falsifiability*, this being interpreted as *derivability* of the negation from a class of observation statements; or on some more complicated deductive relationship involving existential quantification over subsidiary hypotheses. It is difficult to review these attempts without coming to the conclusion that Hempel drew in 1950,[6] that "it is useless to continue the search for an adequate criterion of testability in terms of deductive relationships to observation sentences."

All of the attempts to formulate the principle of empiricism deductively are disposed of by logically trivial arguments. Hempel argues against *verifiability* and *falsifiability* that they fail to meet his criterion of adequacy that a meaningful whole must have only meaningful parts (for if *p* is verifiable and *q* not, then *p or q* is; if *p* is falsifiable and *q* not, then *p and q* is). Be this as it may, it is clear that neither gets the desired class of statements. There are perfectly meaningful statements of high-level theoretical physics such that neither they nor their denial are *deducible* from observation sentences. The more complicated criteria of Ayer and others, framed in terms of deductive relations involving subsidiary hypotheses, turned out to be almost vacuous. Restriction to syntax, which was thought to be required by the principle of empiricism, made that principle impossible to formulate.

SEMANTICS

By the middle thirties, Tarski had convinced Carnap of the legitimacy of semantics. But acceptance of this point of view was by no means immediate among the logical empiricists. At the International Congress for Scientific Philosophy in 1935 Tarski's theory of truth was attacked by Neurath and others as un-empirical metaphysics. Not everyone was as open-minded as Carnap, and it took some time for the legitimacy of semantics to be generally accepted. Even among those who did accept it, it took some time to arrive at a thoroughly semantical point of view. Old habits of thought die hard. For a long time Carnap persisted in doing semantics in a kind of syntactical way, i.e., he did everything in terms of state-descriptions (maximally specific *sentences*) rather than states of affairs or models. (One cannot help noticing that even Tarski himself takes a more syntactical approach in the *Wahrheitsbegriff*[7] than in *Undecidable Theories*.[8] That is, in the *Wahrheitsbegriff* Tarski devotes most of the discussion to giving an *explicit definition* of truth from which all the Tarski biconditionals are *deducible*, whereas in *Undecidable Theories* the focus [in Tarski's theorem] is on getting the extension of the truth predicate right.)

The legitimacy of semantics is a very liberating idea, and philosophy is, in various ways, still exploring the territory that it opened up. For instance, the emphasis on semantics shifts attention from syntactic definability to questions of whether extensions of a set of terms determine the extension of a term under investigation, and if so, how. (It is only in very special circumstances that the two sets of questions coincide.) Thus, we are first directed to the basic question of *supervenience*. In mind-body debates a physicalist can retreat from quixotic promises of explicit definability sometime in the future to the position that a complete physical specification of the body determines the mental state. Or, to take a rather different example, in the Stalnaker-Lewis semantics for subjunctive conditionals, the truth of subjunctives is *supervenient* on the truth values of non-subjunctive propositions. Then again, we can investigate not just denotation but denotation at some index point: e.g., a place or a time. In this sense, we can have a semantical analysis of a tensed language carried out in a non-tensed metalanguage, or a semantical analysis of a modal language carried out in an extensional metalanguage. Analyses of this kind have been at the center of recent philosophical logic. To move in a slightly different direction, we might be interested in some cases not so much in the actual denotations in a model, as rather in their *structure vis-à-vis* one another or *vis-à-vis* both one another and also the denotations of some other terms whose actual denotation we *do* find crucial. This focus on semantical structure is at the heart of the Ramsey sentence approach to theoretical terms in science, and of at least one version of *functionalism* in the mind-body debates.

The semantical point of view suggests reformulation of the principle of empiricism. There are, of course, the semantical analogues of the syntactical attempts: substituting logical consequence for derivability. These are not much better than the syntactical formulations they replaced. They are *somewhat* better because of the problem of capturing the mathematics of a well-developed science. Even at the level of arithmetic we know that if we stay in a first-order language where derivability and logical consequence coincide, there will be unintended non-standard models. If, on the other hand, we move to a richer second-order language to rule out the nonstandard models, derivability no longer captures logical consequence. So we really *must* move to the semantical level to capture the deductive relationships the positivists had in mind when discussing verifiability and falsifiability.

What is more interesting is that the semantical viewpoint can lead to new approaches. One is again led naturally to the idea of *supervenience*: that the empirically significant propositions are those whose truth values are determined by the truth values of certain basic propositions whose truth values are observationally determinable. A view of this sort was held by Russell in his logical atomist period.[9] If one thinks that the basic observational propositions can be characterized as atomic propositions which claim that a relation from an appropriate class of observable relations holds for an n-tuple of objects from an appropriate class of observable objects $[R \, o_1 \, .. \, o_n]$ and their denials, then the truth values of the members of the class of observable propositions are determined by, and jointly determine, an *observable model*, $[D, f]$ where D is the domain of observable objects and f is a function assigning to each observable relation an observable extension consisting of a class of n-tuples of observable objects.[10] One can then think of an empirically meaningful proposition as the class of observable models which make it true and of the empirical import of a theory as the class of observable models which can be extended to models of the theory. A theory along these lines has recently been proposed by van Fraassen.[11]

One might investigate the empirically meaningful propositions which are expressible in a given language. If we build up a first-order language from predicates designating empirical relations and names designating empirical objects and quantifiers ranging over empirical objects, we find that the sentences of that language express empirically meaningful propositions; their truth values are determined by the empirical models. In particular, the notion of supervenience has solved the problems that the quantifiers posed for earlier criteria of empirical meaningfulness. Hempel (1950)[12] proposed translatability into such a language as a new criterion of cognitive meaning. However, from the point of view of supervenience, there are many empirically meaningful propositions which are not expressible in such a first-order language. For instance there is the proposition that there are infinitely many observable objects (or indeed that there are uncountably many observable objects). These propositions would be empirically meaningful in the sense of supervenience but not in the sense of translatability into a first-order empiricist language.

But notice that the idea (even in the more generous model-theoretic form) is extremely restrictive. Hempel ultimately rejects it because it leaves reasonable sentences containing disposition terms and theoretical terms out in the cold. A statement attributing a certain charge to the electron would turn out to be empirically meaningless. We need not even go this far for an example. Suppose that our theoretical statement is that a coin is fair and is being flipped in such a way that the tosses are independent, and that our observational model specifies an outcome sequence. Since any outcome sequence is consistent with both the hypothesis and its denial, the hypothesis is not empirically meaningful according to the proposal under consideration. After the early thirties, most of the positivists—certainly Hempel and Carnap—found such a doctrine too restrictive.

Thus we have attempts at liberalization from Carnap's reduction sentences in "Testability and Meaning" (1936)[13] to his treatment of theoretical concepts in "The Methodological Character of Theoretical Concepts" (1956).[14] The shortcomings of these attempts in the end led both Carnap and Hempel to a holistic view of the empirical content of theories. Theories have a partial empirical interpretation, and this empirical content extends to the theoretical terms somehow *via* the structure of the theory. But how? Carnap was attracted to the Ramsey sentence account of theories. For a finitely axiomatizable theory, we take the conjunction of the axioms as the theory sentence T. If we substitute variables for all the theoretical terms in T and prefix the result with existential quantifiers over these variables, we get ^RT, the Ramsey sentence for T. The Ramsey sentence says that there are some objects and relations or other which have the structure *vis-à-vis* one another and *vis-à-vis* the observable objects and relations that the theory says that the objects and relations denoted by the theoretical terms have. Ramsey suggests[15] and Carnap agrees[16] that the Ramsey sentence captures the empirical meaning of the theory. Carnap adds the idea that the rest of the theory is *convention*; that we agree that the objects and relations constituting the appropriate structure (assuming existence and uniqueness) are the ones to which the theoretical terms refer. At high theoretical levels this view can be very persuasive. What could it *mean* to attribute color or flavor to a quark other than to say that it has some property which plays a certain theoretical role? On the other hand we seem to have a grasp on the meaning of lower-level theoretical terms which is somewhat independent of theory.

The Ramsey idea need not be developed at the level of sentences. It can be directly implemented at the level of models.[17] The theory claims that the world contains objects and relations constituting a certain structure within which the objects and relations denoted by the empirical terms of the theory play the specified role. Thus the "Ramsification" of a theory goes beyond the claims of an empirical model to claim the existence of a partly non-observable structure within which it is embedded.

However, despite the real interest of Ramsey's idea, it does not actually advance the problem we have been discussing. For we can "Ramsify" any theory we please, including one containing as much metaphysics as we please, and the resulting Ramsey sentence will then make a structural claim deriving in part from the metaphysics.

The attempts at formulating the principle of empiricism that we have discussed in this section all give sentences which contain theoretical terms a sharply different status from sentences which contain only observational terms. They thus face a delicate task in coming to terms with the notorious vagueness of "observational." Carnap puts the problem succinctly:

> There is no question who is using the term "observable" in a right or proper way. There is a continuum which starts with direct sensory observations and proceeds to enormously complex, indirect methods of observation. Obviously no sharp line can be drawn across this continuum; it is a matter of degree. A philosopher is sure that the sound of his wife's voice, coming from across the room, is an observable. But suppose that he listens to her on the telephone. Is her voice an observable or isn't it? A physicist would certainly say that when he looks at something through an ordinary microscope, he is observing it directly. Is this also the case when he looks at it through an electron microscope? Does he observe the path of a particle when he looks at the track it makes in a bubble chamber? In general, the physicist speaks of observables in a very wide sense compared with the narrow sense of the philosopher, but, in both cases, the line separating the observable from the non-observable is highly arbitrary.[18]

PRAGMATICS

Pragmatics, the study of the relations of signs and their significations to sign users, has too often been used as a kind of garbage category in philosophy. Issues are characterized as "merely pragmatic" when an author wishes to belittle them or at least to avoid thinking about them very carefully. The entry under pragmatics in the *Encyclopedia of Philosophy* reads as follows: "See Semantics." (This is not because there is any thorough treatment of pragmatics in the article on semantics.) Perhaps the tendency toward philosophical neglect of pragmatics stems from the idea that pragmatics, being the study of the relations between signs and their significations to sign users, must end up being psychology or sociology rather than philosophy. If so, it rests in an idea that is clearly mistaken. It is a mistake that Carnap did not make. In his (1963) reply to Morris[19] he agrees that there is an urgent need to develop a pure pragmatics.

There have been developments. In a sense, pragmatics overlaps with semantics when the signification of the sign is the sign user, or is determined by relations to the sign user: e.g. in the semantics of "I," "you," "now," "here," verb tenses, and the like. Considerable work has been done in these areas since Carnap wrote.

In a more full-blooded sense, the theory of speech acts and of conversational implicature from Austin to Grice and Searle constitutes a flowering of informal pragmatic analysis. At a more formal level, the most influential and highly developed area of pure pragmatics is one with which Carnap was familiar: the theory of rational degrees of belief of Ramsey and de Finetti.

Ramsey and de Finetti focused on the role of degrees of belief as part of the logic of rational decision. In determining preferences for risky ventures—and all ventures are risky to some extent—one needs to take into account both one's degrees of belief in the possible outcomes and one's evaluation of their desirability. There are certain natural pragmatic requirements of coherence for such practical reasoning. One should not, for instance, end up preferring A to B, B to C, and C to A. Ramsey and de Finetti showed how various pragmatic requirements of coherence force the degrees of belief involved to conform to the mathematical structure of the calculus of probabilities. This personal probability representation of rational degrees of belief will be discussed in chapter 2. It will form the basis for much of this book.

De Finetti did something more. He offered a kind of pragmatic reduction of statements involving *chance* or physical probability. The reduction is interesting both for what it shows us about chance and as a specimen of a new kind of philosophical reduction. De Finetti does not offer a *translation* of chance. Rather, he looks at the *role* that chance plays in standard statistical reasoning, and argues that that role can be fulfilled perfectly well without the metaphysical assumption that chances exist. Allow me to sketch the argument briefly. How does chance function in standard probabilistic reasoning? If we are uncertain as to the chance of a chancy event, we average out the possible chances, taking as the weights of the average our degrees of belief that the chance in question is the correct chance. For example, a coin is to be tossed. It is either biased two to one in favor of heads, or to the same degree in favor of tails, so the chances are either $2/3$ heads, $1/3$ tails; or $1/3$ heads, $2/3$ tails, you don't know which. Suppose that you consider these alternatives as to what the chances might be equiprobable, assigning to each degree of belief $1/2$. Then your degree of belief for heads on the next toss is $(1/3)(1/2) + (2/3)(1/2) = 1/2$. Rational degree of belief is the *expectation* (or probability-weighted average) of chance. To put the matter in technical terms, chance functions as a *random variable* in the determination of rational degrees of belief. If we have a long series of trials which are independent in the chance distributions, we can update our degrees of belief in what the chances are *via* Bayes' theorem. Over an infinite series of such trials our degrees of belief will almost surely concentrate on one of the chance hypotheses: $\text{Chance}(H) = 1/3$, $\text{Chance}(H) = 2/3$.

De Finetti is the kind of positivist who doesn't believe in chance—who regards the whole idea as metaphysical excess baggage—but still wants to give an account of the kind of Bayesian reasoning referred to in the last paragraph. He gives such an account by proving a famous *representation* theorem. In essence, this shows that *one who has degrees of belief which exhibit a certain symmetry behaves as if he believes in chances and is uncertain as to what the correct chance distribution is.* For de Finetti, this demonstrates that belief in the *reality* of chances is a difference that makes no difference; chances are, for him, simply an artifact of the representation theorem.

De Finetti's representation theorem treats one important special case. To make the argument for chance in general, one would need much more general representation theorems. Such theorems do indeed exist. De Finetti's theorem, finite approximations to it, various generalizations of it, and their import for a general treatment of chance will be discussed in chapter 3.

Now de Finetti's theorem (suitably generalized) would constitute a certain kind of philosophical reduction of chance to rational degree of belief. What kind of reduction would it be? It would not be a *definition* of chance, or a *semantics* for chance, in terms of rational degree of belief. Rather, we see that with respect to the role that chance plays within a framework of rational degrees of belief, chance is dispensable. The reduction is functional and pragmatic. *It would betray a fundamental misunderstanding of this program to object that degrees of belief depend on believers and chances do not.* Degrees of belief putatively about chance depend on believers, and the claim is that we can do just as well without them, relying only on degrees of belief not about chance. In thinking about de Finetti's program we must bear in mind the kind of pragmatic reduction that is being attempted, and be careful not to confuse it with a definitional or semantic reduction.

In fact, a definitional reduction has been attempted by some[20] for the kind of case that de Finetti treats. That is to say that chance *means* limiting relative frequency in an infinite sequence of trials. There is a problem with this. If you believe in chances, you will no doubt say that in this case, although the credibility of chance diverging from limiting relative frequency is zero, this does not mean that it is logically impossible for chance to diverge from limiting relative frequency. A possibility of credibility zero is still a possibility. De Finetti's reply to someone who believes in chance would be that from the standpoint of our credibilities (rational degrees of belief), the hypothesized possibility of credibility zero makes no difference. It does not affect the expectation of chance. From the pragmatic viewpoint, the question of the semantics of chance is thus underdetermined and, in a certain sense, irrelevant.

These questions will be discussed more fully in chapter 3. I hope that enough has been said here to convince the reader that pragmatics and pragmatic analyses do allow a quite different approach from that presumed in syntactical or semantical analyses. What I would like to do now is to ask how the principle of empiricism would look if formulated within the theory of rational degrees of belief.

A PRAGMATIC REFORMULATION OF THE PRINCIPLE OF EMPIRICISM

First, a word about the "rational" in "rational degree of belief." I assume that this carries with it enough constraints to assure a probability representation. Rationality may carry with it further constraints. I want to leave open at this point the question as to how much they narrow down the range of rational probability assignments. This is a parameter of the account to be given.

A confirmability theory of empirical meaningfulness might hold that a proposition has empirical meaning if and only if some evidence weighs for or against it; i.e., if its credibility on that evidence is greater than or less than its credibility unconditionally. By Bayes' theorem, a bit of evidence is relevant to the hypothesis if and only if the hypothesis is relevant to the evidence in the same sense (positive or negative).

$$Pr(H \text{ given } E)/Pr(H) = Pr(E \text{ given } H)/Pr(E)$$

So the intuition is that a hypothesis whose assumption does not influence the credibility of any evidential statement is not empirically meaningful. For example, consider a religious theory to the effect that "Everything that happens, happens by the will of the gods," but which is hedged in such a way that it has no probabilistic predictive or retrodictive value.

Carnap held a credibility theory of meaning something like this.[21] It was put forward within the context of Carnap's program for inductive logic and was perhaps unjustly neglected as that program languished. Here we wish to investigate the idea when it is considered within the theory of personal probability. In this context it takes on a slightly different character.

The foregoing formulation is relative to a probability function, and we want to take seriously the idea that whatever the constraints of rationality may be, they leave open a rich variety of eligible probability functions. Empirical meaningfulness is then empirical meaningfulness for epistemic agent X at time t. *One man's metaphysics may be another man's empirically meaningful proposition.* The proposition that God exists is empirically meaningful for William Paley and for Clarence Darrow, whereas Frederick Schleiermacher and Paul Tillich proudly give it metaphysical status.

This difference between empirically meaningful propositions and metaphysics has an important social aspect. Suppose that a proposition is empirically meaningless for a group of epistemic agents. For example, suppose that there are three agents for each of whom the proposition "Everything that happens, happens by the will of the gods" is empirically meaningless. One, the Believer, assigns the proposition probability .999; another, the Atheist, assigns it probability .001; the third, the Agnostic, assigns it probability .5. Suppose that this community is then exposed to common evidence and that each agent updates his degrees of belief by conditionalizing on the evidence. No matter what the common evidence is, the final probabilities of the Believer, the Atheist, and the Agnostic for the proposition in question will remain .999, .001, and .5 respectively. Here, metaphysics appears as *dogmatism* with the Agnostic being in a way as dogmatic as the Believer or the Atheist. *For metaphysical propositions we do not have the convergence of opinion of a group of epistemic agents under the pressure of common evidence that might normally be expected.*

The emphasis on convergence of opinion also fits well with the "logical" in "logical empiricism." The logical empiricists held that logically true propositions, though not *empirically* meaningful, were nevertheless meaningful in another way. If we take logic as built into the constraints of rational degree of belief such that logical truths must receive probability one in all rational probability assignments, then opinion converges for them simply because it starts out in agreement. Although not *empirically* meaningful, they all receive probability one in the Pierceian limit for every rational epistemic agent. Taking some liberties with the original idea, let us say that a proposition has *a priori* status if all rational probability assignments give it the same probability. Contradictions as well as tautologies have *a priori* status. What other propositions have *a priori* status depends on how stringent the constraints of rationality. A proposition has metaphysical status for X at t if it is neither empirically meaningful for X at t nor *a priori*.

It is interesting to note that on this criterion, an empirically meaningful whole can have empirically meaningless parts.[22] Consider the conjunction of a metaphysical proposition, M, with an empirically meaningful one, E, where each has initial probability $\frac{1}{2}$; suppose that they are independent and independent conditional on all possible evidence. Then the conjunction is empirically meaningful. By definition, there is evidence relevant to the meaningful conjunct, E, which by independence of M and E conditional on the evidence is relevant to the conjunction $M \& E$. However the presence of the metaphysical conjunct is not without its effect. Under the most favorable evidence the conjunction can at best attain only credibility $\frac{1}{2}$, since the final credibility of M must be $\frac{1}{2}$ and $Pr(E \& M)$ is always no greater than $Pr(M)$.

There is another way in which a meaningful whole can contain a metaphysical component which is of interest, and which requires an extension of our treatment. That is as an operator. Consider the sentential operator ∇, where ∇p is to be read as "p and p is so by the will of the gods." Now if p is empirically meaningful, then ∇p may be empirically meaningful because it is sensitive to the evidence *via* p, even though the operator is intuitively metaphysical. The way here to see whether the sensitivity of ∇p to the evidence comes only from p or not is to see whether a ratio of probabilities is sensitive to the evidence: i.e., $Pr(p \,\&\, \nabla p)/Pr(p \,\&\, {}^\neg\nabla p)$. In other words, we focus on a conditional probability; the probability of ∇p conditional on p. If this conditional probability is sensitive to the evidence, then the operator is empirically meaningful. An operator, ∇, has *a priori* or logical status if for all rational probability assignments $Pr(\nabla p)$ is a function of $Pr(p)$. For example, negation has logical or *a priori* status. An operator has metaphysical status if it is neither empirically meaningful nor *a priori*.

An important thing to notice about this criterion of empirical meaningfulness is that it is much more generous than some of the candidates previously surveyed. There is no reason why statements about electrons, quarks, fields, virtual particles, and all sorts of theoretical entities cannot be empirically meaningful for a reasonable epistemic agent. We will see in chapter 3 how statistical theories can be empirically significant in this sense, in a way they could never be on a strict semantical view. We will see in chapter 5 how the Bayesian theory there presented renders subjunctive conditionals empirically significant.

Some metaphysical-sounding things may be empirically significant. A physical-necessity operator may be empirically significant if it is interpreted in certain ways. For instance, if *Necessarily a is F* means that everything like *a* in certain specified ways is *F*, then *Necessarily a is F* may very well be empirically significant.

What would not be empirically significant would be a physical-necessity operator which had the hypothesized status of "And it is so by the will of the gods"; one such that no evidence was relevant to the ratio of the probabilities of *Nec-*

essarily p and *p but not necessarily p*. With respect to statistical theories and statements of chance, something similar
can be said. The statement that the chance of heads is ½ and
the tosses independent can very well be empirically significant while various statements that philosophers make about
chance turn out to be metaphysics. For instance consider the
statement that chances are really "out there" and not supervenient on manifest properties; or the statement that there is
a set of possible worlds in which the chances disagree with
limiting relative frequency (the set having credibility zero).
It is, I think, the metaphysical admixture in "chance" that
de Finetti really objects to, and one way to look at the representation theorem is as an analytical tool for separating the
empirically meaningful component of chance from the metaphysical admixture. Serious consideration of these questions requires an investigation of generalizations of de Finetti's theorem, and of the accounts of learning from
experience that flow from them. We take up these questions
in chapter 3.

Nothing has been said so far to show that metaphysical
propositions must lack truth values. Propositions which are
metaphysical for a person or group of persons may well be
perfectly sensible propositions. This contrasts with the stance
of the Vienna Circle. What is peculiar about metaphysics
from our standpoint is that it is neither *a priori* by the constraints of rational belief nor sensitive to the pressure of the
evidence. Suppose that an epistemic agent assigns a proposition high probability independent of all evidence, and that
high probability is not dictated by the constraints of rational
belief, whatever they may be. Suppose that the proposition
happens to be true. Does his true belief qualify as knowledge? I don't think so. Even if everything that happens does
happen by the will of the gods, the Believer didn't *know* it.
His belief has no more cognitive validity than the Atheist's
disbelief or the Agnostic's "suspension(?)" of belief. It is based
on neither reason nor experience.

The pragmatic analysis of empirical meaningfulness, then,
leads to the conclusion that metaphysics isn't knowledge. If

so, we can echo the epigraph from Hempel with a slight modification: "All non–*a priori knowledge* is based on experience." The positivists were onto something fundamental with the verification principle, but they misidentified it. Knowability was conflated with meaningfulness; epistemology with semantics. When transposed to its proper pragmatic setting, the verification principle can be seen as a truism elucidating the concept of knowledge. True belief without the support of evidence or reason is not knowledge. The old objection that the verification principle is self-refuting loses whatever force it had. The principle of empiricism is an *a priori* truth of reason and a cornerstone of the theory of knowledge.

2 Degrees of Belief

. . . the wise man follows many things probable that he has not grasped nor perceived nor assented to but that possess verisimilitude.

Cicero
Academica

Rational belief comes in various strengths, a fact that is most dramatic when grounds for belief are equivocal and the stakes involved are high: e.g., in medicine, jurisprudence, and serious gambling. This did not escape the ancients.[1] Signs which are evidence but not conclusive evidence are discussed by Aristotle in the *Rhetoric*, and by Cicero in many places. When the point is pressed, the gradations become finer and finer, and less and less seems absolutely certain. Careful epistemologists from Carneades in the second century B.C. to J. L. Austin and Wilfred Sellars have concluded that even the immediate evidence of the senses should not bestow absolute certainty. A reasonable theory of rational action and decision must take into account degrees of belief.

The idea of justifying the probability calculus as embodying laws of static coherence for degrees of belief goes back to Ramsey's famous essay "Truth and Probability."[2] Ramsey had the idea that qualitative constraints could lead to a representation theorem for probability. And he had the idea of a Dutch book theorem: a theorem to the effect that if probabilities are taken as betting quotients then someone who violates the laws of the probability calculus would be susceptible to a system of bets, each of which he considers fair or favorable, such that he would suffer a net loss no matter what happened. Since the leading ideas of the Dutch book theorems are remarkably simple, we will discuss them first.

DUTCH BOOK THEOREMS

What do you consider a fair price for a wager which pays $1 if p is true; nothing otherwise? To keep you honest, we can rely on the wisdom of Solomon: You set the price, but I decide whether you buy the bet from me or I buy the bet from you. The price you judge to be fair for this bet we will take[3] as your personal probability for p.

Certain features of personal probability follow immediately: (I) You would be mad to have a personal probability greater than one or less than zero, for in the first case I could sell you the bet for more than you could possibly win, and in the second case I could buy it from you for less than nothing, i.e., you would pay me to take it off your hands. (II) You had best give a tautology, p or not-p, personal probability one and a contradiction, p and not-p, personal probability zero, for a bet on a tautology is a bet that you must win and a bet on a contradiction is a bet that you must lose.

Another property follows almost as quickly. Suppose that you buy (sell) a bet that pays $1 if p but nothing otherwise for $.25 and that you buy (sell) a similar bet on q for $.50 and that p is logically incompatible with q. Then you have, in effect, bought (sold) a bet which pays $1 if p or q but nothing otherwise for $.75. If you are to be consistent, your personal probability for p or q had better be $.75, i.e., probability (p) + probability (q). If it is lower, I could buy a bet on p or q from you at less than $.75 and sell it back to you piecemeal (as bets on p and on q) for $.75. If it is higher, you could be embarrassed by the converse transaction.[4]

That's almost all there is to it. If we pause to survey this simple argument we see that what is basic is the consistency condition that you evaluate a betting arrangement independently of how it is described (e.g., as a bet on p or q or as a system of bets consisting of a bet on p and a bet on q). Ramsey puts it this way:

> If anyone's mental condition violated these laws, his choice would depend on the precise form in which the option were offered him, which would be absurd. He could then have book made against him by a cunning bettor and would then stand to lose in any event.[5]

The cunning bettor is simply a dramatic device—the Dutch book a striking corollary—to emphasize the underlying issue of coherence.

I said that the properties just given a pragmatic justification—(i) probability is non-negative, (ii) probability of a tautology is one, (iii) probability is finitely additive—are *almost* all there is to probability. The standard measure–theoretic treatment of probability due to Kolmogoroff assumes a stronger form of additivity: countable additivity.

Let us assume that the propositions about which we have degrees of belief are closed not only under finite truth functions but also under countable disjunction and conjunction. Let us assume that the probability values are real numbers. We say that our probability function is *countably additive* iff (iv) for a countable disjunction of pairwise mutually incompatible propositions, p_1 or p_2 or . . . ,

$$\Pr(p_1 \text{ or } p_2 \text{ or } \dots) = \Sigma_i \Pr(p_i)$$

[where $\Sigma_i \Pr(p_i)$ is the limit of the sequence of partial sums $\Pr(p_1) + \Pr(p_2) + \dots + \Pr(p_n)$]. Countable additivity is the property which allows the standard measure–theoretic treatment of probability density functions.

Although mathematically convenient, countable additivity has been a matter of some controversy in the foundations of personal probability. De Finetti has opposed it, arguing that a rational agent should be able to believe that the tickets in a denumerably infinite lottery are equally likely to win.

Assuming that probability is real-valued, this is impossible if probability is countably additive for then if the probability of a given ticket winning is greater than zero, the probability that some ticket wins would have to be greater than one. But if the probability of a given ticket winning is zero, then by countable additivity the probability that some ticket wins would have to be zero. Weakening the condition to finite additivity allows that for each ticket, the probability that it wins is zero, while the probability that some ticket wins is one.

Notice, however, that de Finetti's agent leaves himself open to a Dutch book. Bet him $101 against $\frac{1}{2}$ that ticket one wins; $101 against $\frac{1}{2}^n$ that the nth ticket wins. You will be assured of a net winning of at least $100 no matter what happens. Indeed, as more than one person has noticed,[6] the coherence argument works just as well for countable additivity as for finite additivity provided that probability is real-valued and we allow countably infinite systems of bets.

Do I ever take on an infinite number of bets? Suppose that I bet that Achilles will drop out of the race. Let it be a very favorable bet: I gain one unit of value if he drops out and lose nothing otherwise. This is a betting arrangement that is tantamount to a countable number of bets: the bet of nothing against one that he drops out in the first half, the bet of nothing against one that he drops out in the first half of the remaining distance, and so forth. Let p_1 be the proposition that he drops out in the first half,[7] p_2 be the proposition that he drops out at the first half of the remaining distance, and so forth. Then the proposition that he drops out is the countable disjunction, p_1 or p_2 or . . . . (You can't drop out on the finish line. If you reach the finish line, you've finished.) Countable additivity of probability tells us that the probability that he drops out should be equal to $\Sigma_i Pr(p_i)$. We will countenance the consideration of countable disjunctions and countable systems of bets as in the foregoing, and will feel free to use the standard theory of countably-additive real-valued probability.[8]

In the Kolmogoroff version of that theory, conditional probability on a condition with non-zero probability is introduced as:

$$Pr(q \text{ given } p) = Pr(p \& q)/Pr(p) \qquad [Pr(p) \neq 0]$$

But the question may arise as to whether this is the appropriate definition. De Finetti provides an answer of a piece with the rationale for the unconditional probabilities by introducing the notion of a conditional bet. A bet on q conditional on p is called off if p is false. If p is true, it is won or lost depending on the truth value of q. Such a betting arrangement can again be described as the upshot of separate bets on p *and* q and against p with the consequence that coherence requires this definition of conditional probability.[9]

So the *statics* of coherence leads us to model rational degrees of belief as countably additive probability measures with conditional probability for conditions of positive probability being defined in the usual way. The question arises as to whether there is any analogous argument for *changing* degrees of belief. Ramsey strongly suggests that he believes that there is such an argument for updating by conditionalization on the evidence:

> Since an observation changes (in degree at least) my opinion about the fact observed, some of my degrees of belief after the observation are necessarily inconsistent with those I had before. We have therefore to explain exactly how the observation should modify my degrees of belief; obviously if p is the fact observed, my degree of belief in q after the observation should be equal to my degree of belief in q given p before. . . . When my degrees of belief change in this way we can say that they have been changed consistently by my observation.[10]

Ramsey, however, does not explicitly set out any such argument.

Despite some skeptical doubts about the possibility of such an argument, Dutch book arguments for conditionalization have been given.[11] Suppose that I am about to learn whether a certain proposition, p, is true or false and that I have a rule or disposition to change my degrees of belief in a certain way if I learn that p is true. Prior to finding out whether or not p is true, *my rule or disposition to change my beliefs in a certain way upon learning p is tantamount to having a set of ratios for bets conditional on p.* (Someone can achieve a betting arrangement for a bet on q conditional on p with me just by reserving a sum that he will bet on q with me *after* I change my degrees of belief if p turns out true, and which he will not bet at all if p turns out false.) But we also know from de Finetti's observation that my prior degrees of belief commit me to betting ratios for conditional bets in a different way, with those betting ratios being reflected in the prior conditional probabilities. For these conditional betting ratios to coincide, the degrees of belief that I would move to upon learning p must coincide with those gotten by conditionalization on p.

This observation yields a Dutch book theorem as a corollary. If someone does not change his degrees of belief by conditionalization, then someone who knows how he does change his degrees of belief can exploit the different betting ratios to make a Dutch book conditional on p, which can be turned into an unconditional Dutch book by making an appropriately small sidebet against p.

In this diachronic coherence argument it is again not the cunning opponent that is fundamental but rather the requirement that different ways in which we can be committed to the same conditional bet receive the same evaluation.

The argument does not show that *all* rational changes of belief should be by conditionalization. There might be no proposition within the domain of the agent's degrees of belief that expresses what is learned; and in such a case nothing appropriate to conditionalize on. Only when such a proposition is at hand and is learned with certainty does diachronic coherence require updating by conditionalization.

If degrees of belief have real numerical values which are tied to betting in the way indicated, we have a rationale for the standard Bayesian assumptions that degrees of belief should be represented by a countably additive probability measure which is updated by conditionalization upon learning a proposition with positive prior probability. But our degrees of belief do not in general have precise numerical values. What can we say if we weaken our framework and only assume comparative degrees of belief, or preferences instead of expected utilities?

REPRESENTATION THEOREMS

A relational structure is said to have a *representation* in some domain of mathematical objects if there is some mapping of the objects and relations of the relational structure onto the mathematical objects and their relations which preserves structure. For example, if my relational structure contains three objects, Sam, Tom, and Sue, and specifies the relation of being *at least as tall as* such that Sam and Sue are at least as tall as each other and neither is at least as tall as Sam and such that the relation is a total order, then one numerical representation would map Sam and Sue both onto 67, Tom onto 72, and at *least as tall* onto *greater than or equal to.* Obviously, there are many other numerical representations as well. A rich enough structure may determine a unique representation, or one that is unique up to a tight group of transformations, but in general representations are underdetermined.

Ramsey had the idea of starting with the qualitative ordering of preference on gambles and extracting a probability-utility representation, an assignment of probabilities and utilities such that the expected utilities that they give order the gambles in the same way as the original ordering. Again, the leading ideas are remarkably simple.

Suppose that you prefer champagne to beer with a Chinese meal but are indifferent between the gambles: (a) Champagne if this coin comes up heads, beer otherwise; (b) Beer if this coin comes up heads, champagne otherwise. Then we might reasonably infer that you take it to be no more likely that the coin at issue come up heads than that it come up tails. Likewise, if there are six goods such that your preferences totally order them with no ties, and you are indifferent between all gambles which assign exactly one of them to each of the faces of a certain die (i.e., your preferences are invariant under permutations of the die faces), then we may reasonably conclude that you take each face of the die to be equiprobable.

The foregoing interpretation depends on the outcome of the flip of the coin or the toss of the die itself not mattering to you. It has no value for you in and of itself, nor does it in any way affect the value of the goods which do matter. Ramsey calls such propositions as "The coin comes up heads" *ethically neutral*. Your ethically neutral propositions are identifiable from your preference ranking in that you are indifferent between payoffs consisting of maximal collections of goods (possible worlds, if you please) which differ only with respect to ethically neutral propositions.

A rich enough set of preferences leads to a set of ethically neutral propositions with arbitrary probabilities. These, in turn, can be used to determine a utility scale. Suppose that your most preferred payoff, TOP, is arbitrarily given utility of 1 and your least preferred alternative, BOTTOM, is given utility of zero. Then a wager *TOP if p, otherwise BOTTOM*, where p is ethically neutral will have a utility equal to the probability of *p*, as will any wager ranked equally with it. Anything preferred to it will have a greater utility; anything to which it is preferred will have a lesser utility. In this way, the probability scale on ethically neutral propositions determines a utility scale on all gambles. Given these utilities one can solve for the probabilities of propositions which are not ethically neutral.

The foregoing sketch of Ramsey's leading ideas is here only to give the uninitiated reader some idea of one natural path from preferences to probability and utility. There are many different ways to such representation theorems, among which are those of Savage, Bolker, and Luce and Krantz.[12] Some representation theorems get only a finitely additive probability, but it is possible to get a representation theorem that yields a countably additive probability (e.g., Bolker) by imposing a continuity condition on preferences.

In all the representation theorems available, the conditions put on preferences to arrive at the representation fall into two groups: the first being fairly intuitive consistency conditions on preferences (e.g., Nothing is preferred to itself. If A is preferred to B and B to C, then A is preferred to C, etc.), and the second being structural conditions which guarantee that the preferences are over a rich enough domain to peg the probabilities and utilities (e.g., that there be enough of the appropriate gambles involving ethically neutral propositions).

Structural richness properties guarantee the uniqueness properties of the representation. (In most approaches the probabilities are determined uniquely and the utilities are determined up to choice of origin and unit; Bolker's result is slightly different.) Thus, on Ramsey's approach, we would like there to be enough gambles on ethically neutral propositions so that we could subdivide the world as finely as we please into equiprobable ethically neutral propositions.

With regard to a similar condition put forward by de Finetti, Savage has this to say:

> It might fairly be objected that such a postulate would be flagrantly *ad hoc*. On the other hand, such a postulate could be made relatively acceptable by observing that it will obtain if, for example, in all the world there is a coin that the person is firmly convinced is fair, that is, a coin such that any finite sequence of heads and tails is for him no more probable than any other sequence of the same length; though such a coin is, to be sure, a considerable idealization.[13]

What are we to make of such simple and attractive idealizations?

We do not, I trust, want to maintain that any rational person must believe that there is such a coin, or indeed that any rational person have a very rich structure of preferences at all. Rather, I believe that we should follow Brian Ellis[14] in interpreting structural richness conditions as *embeddibility* conditions. A rational system of preferences need not be rich, but it should be able to grow. It should not preclude expansion, e.g., by addition of a gamble contingent on an independent flip of a fair coin. If we are willing to say this, then by iterated expansion we have as a condition of rationality embeddibility in the sort of rich system of preferences which gives us the representation theorem. Then rational systems of preferences will have a probability-utility representation.

What we lose, by taking this viewpoint, is the uniqueness of the representation. A system of preferences over a modest domain which is embeddible in a rich system of preferences will typically be embeddible in more than one such system. It will therefore have not one probability-utility representation but rather a set of probability-utility representations. This is, I think, a virtue rather than a defect of the embeddibility approach. It gives a more realistic picture of a decision maker—one that does not assume that people have unique precise probability assignments—while at the same time licensing the analytical techniques of the probability calculus and utility theory.

HIGHER-ORDER DEGREES OF BELIEF

It is hardly in dispute that people have beliefs about their beliefs. Thus, if we distinguish degrees of belief, we should not shrink from saying that people have degrees of belief about their degrees of belief. Nevertheless, the founding fathers of the theory of personal probability are strangely reticent about extending that theory to probabilities of a higher order. Ramsey does not consider the possibility. De Finetti rejects it. Savage toys with the idea but decides against it. This reticence is, I think, ill-founded.

That the mathematics is at hand to treat probabilities of probabilities should not be in question. The mathematical treatment of probability as a random variable is familiar from standard examples of uncertain chances. And as we will see in the next chapter, ordinary first-order probabilities may be tantamount to such a set-up. De Finetti's representation theorem for exchangeable sequences is, among other things, a consistency proof for taking probability as a random variable. Some writers who claim that dealing with probabilities of probabilities leads to inconsistency prove, on examination, to be simply confused.[15]

One might however hold that although formally consistent, a theory of higher-order *personal* probabilities is, in some way, *philosophically* incoherent. This appears to be de Finetti's position. He adopts an *emotive* theory of probability attribution:

> Any assertion concerning probabilities of events is merely the expression of somebody's opinion and not itself an event. There is no meaning, therefore, in asking whether such an assertion is true or false or more or less probable.

> Speaking of unknown probabilities must be forbidden as meaningless.[16]

If probability attribution statements are merely ways of evincing degrees of belief, they do not express genuine propositions and are not capable themselves of standing as objects of belief.

De Finetti's positivism stands in sharp contrast to Ramsey's pragmatism:

> There are, I think, two ways in which we can begin. We can, in the first place, suppose that a degree of belief is something perceptible by its owner; for instance that beliefs differ in the intensity of a feeling by which they are accompanied, which might be called a belief-feeling of conviction, and that by degree of belief we mean the intensity of this feeling. This view . . . seems to me observably false, for the beliefs we hold most strongly are often accompanied by practically no feeling at all.

> We are driven therefore to the second supposition that the degree of belief is a causal property of it, which we can express vaguely as the extent to which we are prepared to act on it.

> The kind of measurement of belief with which probability is concerned is . . . a measurement of belief *qua* basis of action.[17]

For Ramsey, then, a probability attribution is a theoretical claim. It is evident that on Ramsey's conception of personal probability, higher-order personal probabilities are permitted (and indeed required).

Even from de Finetti's viewpoint, the situation is more favorable to a theory of higher-order personal probabilities than might at first appear. For a given person and time there must *be*, after all, a proposition to the effect that that person has the degree of belief that he might evince by uttering a certain probability attribution statement. De Finetti grants as much:

> The situation is different, of course, if we are concerned not with the assertion itself but with whether "someone holds or expresses such an opinion or acts according to it," for this is a real event or proposition.[18]

With this, de Finetti grants the existence of propositions on which a theory of higher-order personal probabilities can be built, but never follows up this possibility.

Perhaps this is because of another sort of philosophical objection to higher-order personal probabilities which, I think, is akin to the former in philosophical presupposition, though not in substance. Higher-order personal probabilities are well-defined, all right—so this line goes—but they are trivial; they only take on the values zero and one. According to this story, personal probabilities—if they exist at all—are directly open to introspection so that one should be certain about their values. If my degree of belief in p is x, then my degree of belief that my degree of belief in p is x will be one; and my degree of belief that my degree of belief is unequal to x will be zero. Put so baldly, the objection seems a bit silly, but I will discuss it because I think that something like it often hovers in the background of discussions of personal probability. But first I would like to point out that this objection has much narrower scope than the previous one. According to this view, it is perfectly all right to postulate non-trivial personal probabilities about personal probabilities if they are my probabilities now about your probabilities now, or my probabilities now about my probabilities yesterday, or tomorrow, or whenever the results of the experiments we are running come in. What become trivial, according to this view, are my probabilities now about my probabilities (that I am introspecting) now.

But even this seems bad psychology and bad epistemology. And if we follow Ramsey in focusing on degrees of belief *qua* basis of action rather than the intensity of feeling notion, the objection vanishes entirely. For in this sense of belief it is entirely possible for a person not to *know his own mind* with certainty.[19]

Given that the conception of higher-order personal probabilities is philosophically legitimate and non-trivial, the question remains as to whether they are of any special interest. Savage's brief discussion in *The Foundations of Statistics* is along these lines:

> To approach the matter in a somewhat different way, there seem to be some probability relations about which we feel relatively "sure" as compared with others. When our opinions, as reflected in real or envisaged action, are inconsistent, we sacrifice the unsure opinions to the sure ones. The notion of "sure" and "unsure" introduced is vague, and my complaint is precisely that neither the theory of personal probability, as it is developed in this book, nor any other device known to me renders the notion less vague. There is some temptation to introduce probabilities of the second order so that a person would find himself saying such things as "the probability that B is more probable than C is greater than the probability that F is more probable than G." But such a program seems to meet insurmountable difficulties. The first of these—pointed out to me by Max Woodbury—is this. If the primary probability of an event B were a random variable b with respect to the secondary probability, then B would have a "composite" probability by which I mean the (secondary) expectation of b. Composite probability would then play the allegedly villainous role that secondary probability was intended to obviate, and nothing would have been accomplished.
>
> Again, once second order probabilities have been introduced, the introduction of an endless hierarchy seems inescapable. Such a hierarchy seems very difficult to interpret, and it seems to make the theory less realistic, not more.[20]

In this passage, Savage seems to have two rather different motivations in mind for higher-order probabilities. The first is the consideration that he begins with—that there is a second-order aspect to our beliefs, i.e., "sureness" about our first-order beliefs, which is not adequately reflected in the first-order probability distribution alone. The second is the idea that second-order distributions might be a *tool* for representing vague, fuzzy, or ill-defined first-order degrees of belief with greater psychological realism than a first-order account alone would provide. The second motivation is implicit in the discussion of the insuperable difficulties, and is made explicit in a footnote in the second edition.[21]

I think that it is very important to carefully distinguish these two lines of thought. Savage's "insuperable difficulties" are serious objections against the suggestion that second-order distributions provide a good mathematical representation of vague, fuzzy, or ill-defined first-order beliefs. Indeed, an apparatus of second-order distributions presumes more structure rather than less. But *however* we wish to treat vague or fuzzy first-order degrees of belief, we shall, given beliefs about beliefs, wish to treat vague or fuzzy second-order degrees of belief as well.

In particular, the treatment of imprecise first-order degrees of belief as represented by a *set* of precise representations is not *in competition* with second-order probabilities; it is aimed at a different problem. If we return to Savage's first motivation, we find that the "insuperable objections" are no longer objections at all. The extra structure of higher-order probabilities is just what is wanted. That two second-order distributions can have the same mean but different variance gives us a representation of the phenomenon with which Savage broached the discussion: Two people may have the same first-order probabilities but different degrees of sureness about them.

If you can be more or less sure about probabilities, you can also be more or less happy about them. That is, there can be *value* associated with propositions of probability. In particular, it is possible for there to be genuine *disutility of risk*. On a first-order approach apparent disutility of risk must be explained as an illusion, generated by the diminishing marginal utility of money.

For example, I prefer no bet to wagering $1,000 on the flip of a coin because the loss of $1,000 would hurt more than the gain of $1,000 would help. This explanation of the apparent disutility of risk, due to Daniel Bernoulli,[22] no doubt describes a real phenomenon, but many from Bernoulli's time to ours have not been able to believe that it is the whole story.[23] Now it is certainly coherent to ascribe a negative value to "butterflies in the stomach" and if an agent believes that the second bet will certainly lead to them, its real consequences are either "Win $1,000 with gastrointestinal upset" or "Lose $1,000 with gastrointestinal upset." So the second bet can in this way have a smaller expected utility than the first even if the marginal utility of money is constant. In like manner, if there is a proposition (or a family of propositions) in our language specifying riskiness (or "ambiguity") of a wager, it is coherent to attach negative or positive utility to riskiness (or "ambiguity") according to one's temperament. We can have such propositions if we have probability as a random variable, with the operative sense of risk depending on the exact interpretation of that random variable. Extending the theory of personal probabilities to higher-order probabilities thus gives one a richer framework within which it is possible, within the constraints of coherence, to give a responsive answer to one of the most persistent criticisms of that theory.

There is one further point in the passage from Savage that invites comment. Savage speculates that the notion of sureness may give some insight into probability change, and indeed the introduction of higher-order degrees of belief does that as well. Our consideration of probability change so far has focused on the rationale for conditionalization; for taking our new probabilities as our old probabilities conditional on the evidence. This gives the evidence probability one. But the assumption that every observation can be interpreted as conferring certainty on some observational proposition appears to lead to an unacceptable epistemology of the given.

There is, however, another way in which conditionalization can be brought to bear via higher-order degrees of belief.

When our epistemic inputs give each first-order proposition a less-than-certain probability, they may nevertheless sometimes be plausibly characterizable as learning (for certain) *that* a proposition has a less-than-certain probability. We can then conditionalize on such a probabilistic proposition.

Rules that appear to be *ad hoc* extensions of conditionalization in a first-order setting can be evaluated as special cases of conditionalization within the framework of higher-order probabilities. For instance, suppose observation raises the probability of a p from .6 to .9. Following Jeffrey[24] we say that observation changes my degrees of belief by *probability kinematics* on the partition $[p, \sim p]$, just in case the probabilities conditional on p and on $\sim p$ remain the same. From the second-order point of view, let us assume that what we learned was that $pr(p) = .9$, and conditionalize on that proposition. It can then be shown that second-order conditionalization yields first-order probability kinematics under a simple hypothesis of conditional independence.[25] That is that for every first-order proposition, q, $PR(q$ given p & $pr(p) = a) = PR(q$ given $p)$ and $PR(q$ given $\sim p$ & $pr(p) = a) = PR$ $(q$ given $\sim p)$. This result can be generalized, and the general approach can be extended to analyze other first-order generalizations of conditionalization.[26] Once higher-order degrees of belief are in hand we can conditionalize on a rich variety of propositions: the proposition that the probability of p is within a certain interval; the proposition that the expectation of any random variable is within a certain interval; conjunctions of the foregoing types of proposition; and so forth. The theory of conditionalization can therefore become a much more comprehensive and powerful theory of rational belief change.

Once we have gone this far, there is no reason why not to consider beliefs about beliefs about beliefs, and so on as far as we please. But there is no reason to view this Bayesian hierarchy as vicious. It provides a very rich framework within which to work. For any practical problem we can utilize as much of it as we need.

In the nearly thirty years since the publication of *The*

Foundations of Statistics, statisticians *have* worked in hierarchical models. I. J. Good[27] considers mixed hierarchies which contain physical and other notions of probability as well as degrees of belief. In comments on a review article by Good, DeGroot remarks:

> I strongly agree with Professor Good about the importance and usefulness of hierarchical models. However, I do not see any need to consider physical logical and subjective probabilities. Subjective probabilities would seem to be enough; they unify the theory and are usually convenient to use.[28]

The implied dispensability of physical probabilities is a reference to de Finetti's theorem and generalizations thereof that we will discuss in the next chapter. For more details about statistics and Bayesian hierarchies, I will have to refer the reader to the literature.[29] Enough has perhaps been said to show how a hierarchy allows a Bayesian a much more inclusive theory of rational belief change than might at first seem possible.

CONCLUSION

Here then, we have the full Bayesian framework of rational degrees of belief together with the leading ideas for its justification. I would not want to hold the framework above criticism, but its foundations compare favorably with most of what passes as epistemology. Careful criticism is more likely to call for modification or generalization than for junking the whole approach. (We will discuss the possibility of some modifications in the chapter on causal decision theory.) For now, let us provisionally adopt the framework and pursue the questions of empiricism from within it.

3 Learning from Experience

Aptly did Plato call natural science the science of the probable.[1]

Simplicius
in Arist. Phys.

. . . inductive reasoning is reduced in this way to Hume's justification.

Bruno de Finetti
"On the Condition of Partial Exchangeability"

COIN FLIPS AND THE UNIFORMITY OF NATURE

Consideration of induction in a non-probabilistic setting might lead one to conclude that scientific inductive logic must presume that nature is *uniform* with the future resembling the past and the unexamined resembling the examined, rather than *random* like the outcome of independent flips of a coin,

This chapter is largely drawn from my "Presuppositions of Induction," forthcoming in a festschrift for Arthur Burks (ed. M. Salmon), and read at the University of Western Ontario, the University of Chicago, Princeton University, the University of Southern California, and the 1982 Pacific Division Meetings of the American Philosophical Association. The research on which it is based was partially supported by National Science Foundation grant SES-8007884.

or willfully *perverse* like a clever opponent in a zero-sum game.

A closer examination of objective uniformity reveals unexpected complications. Postulation of uniformity means nothing unless we specify the respects in which uniformity is postulated. Uniformity is relative to a system of classification. This basic insight was already there, submerged in the chorus line, with Hume and Mill.[2] Nelson Goodman brought it to center stage with such glamor[3] that it dazzled the eye.

There are complications even if we abstract away Goodman's problem. Suppose that we consider a sequence of outcomes of the same experiment, assuming that the notion of "same experiment" and the outcome space have been chosen with an eye toward projectibility. The question arises as to what we are to count as a uniform sequence; or better, as a sequence with some degree of uniformity. One is naturally led to the consideration of *random* sequences as the really non-uniform ones.

What are the random sequences? Well, the random process consisting of a sequence of independent and identically distributed trials (like the coin tosses) should have a high probability[4] of producing random sequences. But this still leaves open a variety of possible definitions. There is an extensive mathematical literature on the characterization of random sequences; it is by no means a trivial question either mathematically or philosophically. Without pursuing the matter in detail, I want to note a fact that is invariant over questions of fine tuning the analysis. It is that random sequences *must* have a limiting relative frequency.[5] This is a rather spicy revelation in view of Reichenbach's taking the existence of limiting relative frequencies as the principle of the uniformity of nature. The most chaotic and disordered alternative to uniformity that we can find *entails* uniformity-in-the-sense-of-Reichenbach! The naive intuition of a dichotomy between randomness and order needs to be qualified. Randomness is indeed a kind of disorder, but it carries with it of necessity a kind of statistical order in the large. If randomness is taken as a standard of non-uniformity, then postulation of this type of non-uniformity is postulation of the existence of limiting relative frequencies.

I haven't said anything yet about the third *prima facie* possibility of nature as a willfully perverse opponent. Certainly the world could be so arranged that its creatures with fixed finite intelligence could be frustrated at every turn. Put in this way there is simply no answer to Hume's problem. It is, however, worth noting that if the capabilities of nature's opponents knew no bounds, then the best a perverse nature could do is adopt a random strategy.

Now what I have been building up to is that the whole question takes on a quite different complexion when considered in the context of rational degrees of belief.

Consider one of the oldest illustrations in the business[6]: A biased coin is to be flipped a number of times. There are two hypotheses about the physical probabilities or chances which characterize the process: the hypothesis that the coin is biased two to one in favor of heads and the tosses are independent (BH); and the hypothesis that the coin is biased two to one in favor of tails and the tosses are independent (BT).[7] Suppose that we believe that these are the only two possibilities with non-negligible probability and that they are equally likely. We assign them each epistemic probability ½. Then it is reasonable that we take as our epistemic probabilities of outcomes an average of their physical probabilities on each hypothesis, with the weights of the average (in this case equal) being the epistemic probabilities of the corresponding hypotheses being correct. So the epistemic probability of heads on toss one is $(½)(⅓) + (½)(⅔) = ½$, likewise for the epistemic probability of heads on toss two. But the epistemic probability of heads on toss two *conditional* on toss one is not ½, but a bit more. Intuitively, this is because the information that the coin comes up heads on toss one supports the hypothesis of bias toward heads a bit more strongly than the hypothesis of bias toward tails. Our elementary example has led us to a philosophical conclusion of fundamental importance. *We can have learning from experience without uniformity of nature.*

In our epistemic probability distribution the proposition

(heads on toss one) has positive statistical relevance to the proposition (heads on toss two) even though we are sure that the tosses are really (*vis-à-vis* the true physical probabilities) independent. Mathematically, this positive statistical relevance is an artifact of the averaging (mixture) of possible chance distributions to come up with our rational degrees of belief. The conditions for learning from experience are here not created by knowledge, but rather by ignorance. Here we are learning from experience not by presupposing that nature is uniform, but rather in the teeth of the conviction that it is not uniform, by virtue of our uncertainty about *how* it is not uniform.

Of course, one might say that we have here uniformity of nature at the level of chance. But I hope that my opening remarks about randomness have cast some doubt on the possibility of belief that nature is not uniform at any level. The discussion of generalized representation theorems later in this chapter will show that belief in uniformity *for some sense of chance or other* is almost inescapable.

With regard to the coin-flip example, it is also worth pointing out that the epistemic probabilities can be represented as a mixture (weighted average) in more than one way. Consider the *relative frequency* distributions corresponding to different possible relative frequencies of heads. Let us construct them so that the outcome sequences giving the same relative frequencies to heads are equally probable.[8] For simplicity, consider the case in which there are only two tosses. Then the relative frequency distributions corresponding to the realizable relative frequencies in such a sequence are:

Relative Frequency of Heads:	1	$\frac{1}{2}$	0
Pr (Heads on 1 & Heads on 2)	1	0	0
Pr (Heads on 1 & Tails on 2)	0	$\frac{1}{2}$	0
Pr (Tails on 1 & Heads on 2)	0	$\frac{1}{2}$	0
Pr (Tails on 1 & Heads on 2)	0	0	1

Each of the columns represents a possible relative frequency distribution. If we average these relative frequency distributions using the epistemic probabilities of the relative frequencies as weights[9] we get back our epistemic distribution. Note here that the relative *frequency* distributions into which we factor the epistemic probability distribution are radically different from the *chance* distributions in terms of which it was represented previously. In the chance distributions, the tosses were independent. But consider the relative frequency distribution corresponding to the relative frequency of heads being ½. In this distribution, the probability of heads on toss 2 is ½, but the probability of heads on toss two conditional on heads on toss one is zero! We have here *negative* statistical relevance with a vengeance. Such distributions (hypergeometric) have been taken as a model[10] for counterinductive reasoning. That is, if I was *sure* that the relative frequency of heads was ½ in a sequence of two tosses, observation of a head on toss one would lead me to drop the probability of a head on toss two from ½ to zero. Obviously the same sort of effect can be illustrated with respect to any finite number of tosses.

We have, in our example, an illustration of three different conceptions of probability: epistemic probability; physical propensity or chance; and relative frequency. Our epistemic probability distributions could be viewed either as a mixture of possible relative frequency distributions or as a mixture of possible propensity distributions, even though the propensity distributions made the trials independent while the relative frequency distributions made an outcome on a trial negatively relevant to the same outcome on another trial. The interaction of these three conceptions of probability lies at the heart of inductive reasoning.

DE FINETTI'S THEOREM

In the preceding section, we took a weighted average to get an epistemic distribution. If we start with the epistemic distribution, we say that it has a *representation as a mixture of* probability distributions. In general, such representations need not be unique. We just saw how this distribution has two quite different representations as mixtures: the mixture of chance distributions and the mixture of relative frequency distributions.

Each of the distributions in the preceding paragraph has the property of being invariant under finite permutations of trials [Pr(Heads on 1 & Tails on 2) = Pr(Tails on 1 & Heads on 2)]. Probability measures with this property are said to make the trials *exchangeable*. Any independent sequence of trials is exchangeable and any mixture[11] of exchangeable sequences (i.e., of probability measures that make the sequences exchangeable) is exchangeable. De Finetti used the concept of exchangeability to prove a representation theorem. It is most neatly put if we consider infinite sequences of trials and assume countable additivity of probability. Then de Finetti's theorem is that an exchangeable sequence of trials has a *unique* representation as a mixture of independent sequences of trials.[12]

De Finetti's theorem establishes a broad domain for the sort of model of learning from experience that we looked at in miniature in the last section. If our degrees of belief are exchangeable, they act as if they were averages of independent chance distributions. We learn from experience just as before. If we observe a sequence of outcomes and conditionalize on that observation, then the subsequence of remaining outcomes is still exchangeable, but the weights of the independent sequences into which it factors will have shifted as a result of our observation. As the sequence of observed outcomes grows, then with probability (degree of belief) approaching one, the weight of the average will become concentrated on one of the independent sequences.[13] Positive statistical relevance between like outcomes of different trials will arise from the averaging, except in the extreme case of a degenerate average where we start out with our degrees of belief already concentrated on one independent sequence. In the case of infinite sequences of trials, de Finetti appears to have replaced the presupposition of the *objective* uniformity of nature with the modest *subjective* condition of exchangeability. Thus, we have de Finetti's sanguine remarks about having resolved the problem of induction along Humean lines. How far de Finetti's theorem goes toward resolving the problem of induction remains to considered. But it cannot be denied that de Finetti's ideas put the problem in a dramatically new light.

The second important thing that de Finetti's thorem does for us is to establish the relationship between the conceptions of degree of belief, relative frequency, and chance in the cases under consideration. Any probability for a finite sequence can be represented as a mixture of those distributions gotten by conditionalizing out on statements of relative frequency. Exchangeability of the original distribution assures that in the factors so obtained all outcome sequence with positive probability are equally probable. Decomposition of finite exchangeable sequences into relative frequency probabilities in this way yields hypergeometric distributions (the "counterinductive," sampling from an urn without replacement type distributions that were the relative frequency distributions of the last section). Every finite exchangeable sequence has a unique representation in this way as a mixture of hypergeometric sequences. As the length of the finite sequence approaches infinity the hypergeometric distribution approaches independence. The factors of the de Finetti representation are gotten by conditionalizing on statements of relative frequency for finite subsequences and passing to the limit.

If we believe that our infinite exchangeable sequence is governed by unknown propensities which make the trials independent, then by the uniqueness clause of de Finetti's theorem we cannot represent our degrees of belief in two materially distinct ways: as a mixture of relative frequency probabilities and as a mixture of physical propensities. That is, the sum of possibilities of disagreement between propensity and relative frequency must have degree of belief zero. It comes to the same thing, whether we think of our sequence as governed by a mixture of propensities or chances, by a mixture of relative frequency probabilities, or simply by an exchangeable degree of belief. De Finetti regards this as a way of dispensing with metaphysically dubious propensities. With regard to our degree-of-belief probabilities, the postulation of propensities pulls no weight.

De Finetti's analysis of the situation is so beautiful that we would almost like to forget that it is a special case. But what if the number of trials is finite? What if the epistemic probabilities are not exchangeable? How far can the bold insights of de Finetti's analysis be generalized?

FINITE EXCHANGEABLE SEQUENCES

In the first section of this chapter, an example was given of a finite exchangeable sequence that could be represented as a mixture in two ways: as a mixture of hypergeometric sequences and as a mixture of independent sequences. Every finite exchangeable sequence has a unique representation as a mixture of hypergeometric sequences, with the elements of the mixture gotten from the original probability by conditioning on statements of relative frequency, and the weights being the respective original probabilities of those relative frequency statements. (E.g., fixing a sequence of coin tosses at length n, we can take the appropriate statements to be: no heads, 1 head, . . . n heads.) Not every finite exchangeable sequence has a representation as a mixture of independent sequences. For instance, consider the hypergeometric distribution in the two-toss case corresponding to one head and one tail.[14]

Those finite exchangeable sequences which do admit a representation as a mixture of independent sequences are of special interest because they are ones which permit learning from experience in the way illustrated in section 1. Under what conditions do we have representability as a mixture of independent sequences in the finite case, or a good approximation to it? There is an illuminating treatment of this question in recent work by Diaconis, and Diaconis and Freedman.[15] They analyze how a finite exchangeable sequence of length r which can be extended to a longer finite exchangeable sequence of length k approximates a mixture of independent sequences, with the error in the approximation going to zero as k approaches infinity. What is important for the finite case is that the analysis yields a bound on the error for finite k which shows that the error disappears fairly fast.[16] We may think it highly likely that an experiment will only be repeated a finite number of times but not be absolutely sure. If we are sure that it will only be repeated a finite number of times, we may be unsure as to how many. Even if we are sure that it can only be repeated r times, we may believe that it could have been repeated a greater number of times and thus have exchangeable beliefs about a sequence of length r that could be extended to exchangeable beliefs about a sequence of longer length k. Diaconis and Freedman take the example of a coin which is flipped only 10 times, where our beliefs are such that they can be extended to an exchangeable sequence of 1,000 flips. Here the error in the representation of the original sequence as a mixture of sequences of 10 independent flips must be no more than .02. There is considerable scope for the application of de Finetti's analysis to finite sequences.

What does this tell us about finite hypergeometric sequences as a model for counterinduction? It should be reemphasized at the onset that hypergeometric sequences are not, in themselves, perverse. If I know that an urn contains 50 red balls and 50 white balls and nothing else, and my experiment consists of random sampling from that urn without replacement, then the hypergeometric distribution is the one that I should adopt. If, after drawing 50 red balls, I change the probability that the 51st draw wil be red to zero, I will have learned from experience in a quite unexceptionable way, notwithstanding the negative statistical relevance of like outcomes on different trials. It is adopting such a distribution in less appropriate circumstances, say in the coin-flipping case, that is perverse.

Concentrating one's probability on a hypergeometric distribution in a case like the coin case, which is more plausibly a mixture of independent distributions, can be taken as a model of counterinductive behavior.[17] Finding a model for a counterinductive *method* may be another matter. Suppose someone believes there will be only 100 tosses of this coin and that exactly half will be heads, and adopts the corresponding hypergeometric distribution as his epistemic probability. What does he predict about the outcome of the 101st toss while the coin is spinning in the air? What probabilities does he assign after observing the 51st heads? There are falsifiable contingent assumptions which lie behind his assignment. They provide no clue as to how the assignment should be extended to a greater number of trials. One might require of a counterinductive *method* that it deal with any possible sequence of observations as input. Diaconis' result then shows just how tightly the counterinductivist is hemmed in by exchangeability.

(This is not to claim that in no sense is a model of counterinductive method possible. The counterinductivist might, at the moment of truth, simply leap to a different hypergeometric distribution consistent with the observations to date, e.g., the one corresponding to an urn with 51 red balls and 50 black balls.[18] This sort of counterinductive strategy would not respect extendability—life would be full of crises requiring leaps to entirely new probability distributions which are not extensions of the old[19] but the counterinductivist is, after all, rather an odd duck anyway.)

Scientific induction has its presuppositions. We do not really need the picture of "the counterinductivist" to dramatize the point. The difficulties encountered in painting the picture are none the less instructive. They emphasize the considerable role of mixing in the creation of statistical relevance in the finite case as well. The theoretical importance of mixtures of independent sequences leads, in the finite case, to a special appreciation of alternative ways of representing a sequence as a mixture. The canonical de Finetti representation as a mixture of relative frequency distributions is, in the finite case, a representation as a mixture of non-independent sequences. In many cases, the same mixture can naturally be represented as a mixture of independent chance sequences. Thus the study of learning from experience in the finite case tends to emphasize the distinction between relative frequency and chance.

STOCHASTIC PROCESSES AND PARTIAL EXCHANGEABILITY

In the theory of stochastic processes, the numbers which index the events are taken to convey information as to some physical order (often temporal order). Here, in the discrete case, we have repetitions of an experiment indexed by the positive integers, or a doubly infinite sequence indexed by the whole numbers (. . . -1, 0, $+1$ . . .), and in the continuous case indexed by a real "time" parameter. (The theory can be generalized so that the experiment is parametrized in several dimensions, in which case we have a *random field*. Random fields form the analytical framework for the study of the statistical mechanics of lattice gases.) Exchangeability in the epistemic distribution and independence in the objective distributions must be considered a special case. However, a great many physical stochastic processes which are not independent satisfy Markov's weakening of independence where the chances of an outcome on a trial depend only on the outcome of the preceding trial. (The Markov property is obviously connected with causality, and an appropriate Markov property in a random field where the parameters represent space and time would represent a probabilistic principle of locality of causation.) It is therefore of great interest whether the de Finetti analysis can be extended to Markov chains. Again, when we are dealing with arbitrary sequences of random variables, rather than just repetitions of an experiment, there is no reason to assume in general that the random variables in question should be exchangeable in the epistemic distribution, or independent in the possible objective distribution.

De Finetti appreciated the importance of these questions from the beginning. In 1937 he wrote: "To get from the case of exchangeability to other cases which are more general but still tractable, we must take up the case where we still encounter 'analogies' among the events under consideration, but without their attaining the limiting case of exchange-ability."[20] To this end, de Finetti introduced the notion of partial exchangeability:

> All the conclusions and formulas which hold for the case of ex-changeability are easily extended to the present case of *partially exchangeable* events which we could define by the same sym-metry condition, specifying that the events divide into a certain number of types 1, 2, . . . g, and that it is only events of the same type which will be treated as "interchangeable" for all probabi-listic purposes. Here again, for this definition to be satisfied quite generally, it need only be satisfied in a seemingly much more special case: it suffices that there be a unique probability ω n_1, n_2, . . . n_g that n given events all happen, where $n_1, n_2 \ldots, n_g$ belong respectively to the first, second, . . . gth types and $n_1 + n_2 + \ldots + n_g = n$—and where this unique probability is indepen-dent of the choice of particular events from each type.[21]

De Finetti introduces this notion of partial exchangeability with a coin-tossing example, where several odd-shaped coins are tossed. Here it is not so plausible to expect exchange-ability in the sequence of all tosses, but it is plausible to expect exchangeability within the sequence of tosses of a given coin. The example can be varied to illustrate various degrees of subjective analogy between the different types of toss. In one limiting case, the coins may be thought to be much the same, with the upshot of this judgment being global exchangeability. As the other end of the spectrum, the coins may be thought so different that the results of tossing one give no information about the bias of the others.

It may not be apparent how this notion of partial ex-changeability is meant to be applied to the theory of stochas-tic processes. The leading idea, in the Markov case, is clear: "In the particular case of events occurring in chronological order, the division into classes may depend on the result of the previous trial; in such a case we have the Markov form of partial exchangeability."[22] That the probability of an out-come on toss 56 of a Markov chain depends on the outcome of toss 55 is not a reflection of any special status of toss 55 over and above its being the predecessor of toss 56. Thus, if we take the subsequence of tosses whose predecessor has a given outcome, renumber them 1, 2, . . . in order of occurrence (thus suppressing some information as to position in the original sequence), we should expect the resulting sequence to be exchangeable.

Even though the leading idea is clear, this case is more complicated than the case of the odd coins, and de Finetti's suggestion constitutes a broadening of the notion of partial exchangeability. To illustrate, consider an example of Diaconis and Freedman.[23] Instead of flipping a coin we flick a thumbtack across the floor, and we play it as it lays. The probability of its landing point up (U) or not may plausibly depend on the result of the previous trial. It would be a mistake to think that we could get an exchangeable subsequence of trials just by conditioning on a statement which posits a fixed outcome (say, point up) for each of their predecessors. Conditioning on the statement that tosses 1, 5, and 6 have predecessors that land point up makes it certain that toss 5 lands point up but cannot be expected to make up on 1 or up on 6 certain. Here the very act of dividing the trials into classes may presuppose information which destroys the exchangeability of the trials within those classes.

On the other hand, there is a generalization from de Finetti's alternative characterization of exchangeability. We can almost give a frequentist characterization of a sequence, so that this characterization can plausibly be held to determine uniquely the probability of that sequence. That is, we can specify the frequency of transitions from state to state (up to up, up to down, etc.) in the sequence. I said "almost" because to this, we must add the non-frequentist information of the initial state of the system.[24] Given that we believe that the probabilities are governed by a Markov law, sequences with the same initial state and the same transition count should be equiprobable.

Freedman, in 1962,[25] brought exchangeability and various forms of partial exchangeability together under the concept of a certain form of sufficient statistic. Let a statistic here be a function from sequences of length n into some set of values (which may be a set of vectors). We say that the statistic, T, is a *summarizing statistic* for the probability assignment, P, on sequences of length n; or alternatively, that the probability assignment is *partially exchangeable with respect to the statistic* iff $T(x) = T(y)$ implies $P(x) = P(y)$ where x and y are sequences of length n. As Diaconis and Freedman[26] point out, this covers all the intended cases of partial exchangeability. In the case of exchangeability, the summarizing statistic consists just of the frequencies (or relative frequencies) of outcomes. In the case of tossing several funny coins and analogous cases, the value of the summarizing statistic consists of a vector whose components are the frequencies (or relative frequencies) for each coin. In the Markov case, we have a vector whose components are the transition counts together with the outcome of the first trial.

Although these two applications are much in the spirit of de Finetti's original analysis, the notion of partial exchangeability with respect to a statistic is a very substantial generalization of the notion of partial exchangeability. In particular, it should be noted that there is nothing in the definition of a summarizing statistic that requires it to be or involve a frequency count. Freedman's treatment moves us very far toward the higher levels of generality that will be discussed in the subsequent sections.

If the statistic, T, is a *summarizing statistic* for two probability assignments P_1 and P_2, then, by definition, for any value of the statistic, the sequences in its inverse image are given the same value by P_1 and likewise for P_2. Those sequences will therefore be given the same value by any weighted average of P_1 and P_2. That is, partial exchangeability with respect to a fixed statistic T is a property of probability distributions preserved by mixing. If we consider the family of probability assignments (on a given set of sequences of length n) which are partially exchangeable with respect to T, it is closed under mixing.[27] Those probability measures which concentrate probability one on the set of sequences which are the inverse image of one value of the statistic are the extreme points of the set of measures, i.e., the ones that cannot be represented as a non-degenerate[28] mixture of distinct measures in the set. If the set contains a regular assignment (one which gives each possible outcome non-zero probability), then all the extremal probability assignments can be recovered from it by conditioning on the possible values of the statistic. We now have the following generalization of de Finetti's theorem for finite sequences:

Every probability assignment P which is partially exchangeable with respect to T is a unique mixture of the extreme measures P_i. The mixing weights are $w_i = P\{x:T(x) = t_i\}$. [Diaconis and Freedman, 1980]

(For a discussion of the extreme measures in the finite case for some of the special cases of partial exchangeability that have been mentioned, see Diaconis and Freedman.)[29]

Freedman (1962) proves a general representation theorem for partial exchangeability with respect to a statistic. Since this concept is defined with respect to finite sequences, it is necessary to find a way to relate the various summarizing statistics for subsequences of an infinite sequence. For our probability space with infinite sequence as its elements, let us take as our new sense of summarizing statistic an infinite sequence of summarizing statistics in the old sense. That is, a statistic, U, in the new sense can be taken as a function from the integers to statistics in the old sense for finite sequences, and a summarizing statistic in the new sense is one such that for any n, U_n, is such that if two finite sequences have the same value of U_n the set of infinite sequences that has them as subsequences in a specified position must be equiprobable. Freedman introduced the notion of an S-structure to assure that the U_ns mesh together nicely. U has an S-structure iff for any finite sequences A, A' of length n and B, B' of length m, if $U_n(A) = U_n(A')$ and $U_m(B) = U_m(B')$ then $U_{n+m}(A @ B) = U_{n+m}(A' @ B')$, where $A @ B$ is the result of concatenating the sequence A with the sequence B. The summarizing statistics mentioned specifically in this section (relative frequency, frequency within types, initial outcome together with transition counts) all have an S-structure. Freedman then proves that a probability P is partially exchangeable with respect to (is summarized by) a statistic U with an S-structure if and only if it has a representation as a mixture of ergodic (metrically transitive) probabilities which are partially exchangeable with respect to U. (I will postpone the discussion of ergodic measures until the next section.) He uses this result to attack the question of the characterization of mixtures of Markov chains. The answer when the stochastic process is stationary is in Freedman (1962). Diaconis and Freedman (1980b)[30] show that when a stochastic process is recurrent[31] it has a representation as a mixture of Markov chains if and only if it is partially exchangeable with respect to the statistic of initial state and transition count. The representation is unique.

In the simpler case of partial exchangeability (several different biased coins), a representation as a mixture of products of Bernoullian measures is given in de Finetti (1938),[32] Link (1980),[33] and Diaconis and Freedman (1980).[34] Link gives proofs of representation theorems for such "k-fold partial exchangeability" using Choquet's theorem as the main analytical tool. Diaconis and Freedman indicate how the proof of one of these theorems can be gotten by passing to the limit in the finite case.

On the other hand, when random processes are generalized to random fields, there are generalizations of de Finetti's theorem. This is an area of much current interest, largely because of the connections with statistical mechanics and thermodynamics. Two recent studies are Preston[35] and Georgii.[36]

It is clear that methods in the spirit of de Finetti can be used to give an analogous account of a more general class of cases than those treated in de Finetti's original theorem. The question as to how general that class in fact is has an answer which depends in part on ongoing mathematical research and in part on how generously we interpret "analogous" and "in the spirit of de Finetti." The consequences of a generous interpretation will be discussed in the next two sections.

INVARIANCE, RESILIENCY, AND ERGODICITY

Many of us would like to think of physical probabilities quite generally in the way that de Finetti thinks of the factors in his theorem; as an artifact of our representation of the epistemic probabilities as a mixture. What is needed to back up such a position is a general mathematical theory. Ideally such a theory should do two things for us. First, it should prove a unique representation theorem. That is, given degrees of belief about the outcome of an experiment (which might be required to be invariant provided that the basic experimental arrangement is fixed), we would like to have a unique representation of our degrees of belief as a mixture of physical probabilities. Second, we would like to have an account of learning from experience. This could be provided if we could prove some kind of law of large numbers for repetitions of an experiment. If we had such an account, we could show how to learn the correct physical probabilities from an experiment, and how it is possible to use the correct physical probabilities to predict the results of a sequence of experiments. Finally we, or at least I, would like to claim that the "objective physical probabilities" should have an objective *resiliency* or invariance under conditionalization, which is connected with the subjective invariance of the degrees of belief with which we started.

Let me formulate these desiderata for the mathematics of a subjectivist theory of chance precisely at a high level of generality. Let our degrees of belief be represented by a probability measure, P, on a standard Borel space (Ω, F, P),[37] where Ω is a set, F is a sigma-field of measurable subsets of Ω, and P is a probability measure on F. We will think of a point in Ω as specifying not only the outcome of an experiment but also the experimental arrangement and background conditions of the experiment. Although we may not know exactly what the physical probabilities are, we may know that some of the background conditions (e.g., time of experiment) are irrelevant to them. That is, the physical probabilities should be invariant under variation of some background conditions and so should the epistemic probability that is a mixture of the possible physical probabilities. We may typically expect that there may be some such symmetry or invariance which characterizes our epistemic probabilities. This may be expressed formally by introducing a transformation (e.g., shift in time of the experiment) which maps the prob-

ability space, Ω, into itself. (We should require that the transformation respect measurability, i.e., that the inverse image
of a measurable set be measurable.) We will then say that our
probability, P, is *invariant with respect to the transformation*, T, if for every measurable set A, a set which the transformation carries into it, $T^{-1}A$, has the same probability that
it does: $P(T^{-1}A) = P(A)$. Invariance with respect to a fixed
transformation is a property of probability measures that is
preserved under mixing.

We know that some background factors are irrelevant to
the physical probabilities, and this information manifests
itself as invariance of epistemic probabilities with respect to
some transformation, T. But we may not know the true values of the relevant variables, so we are uncertain about the
correct physical probabilities. We want to think of the possible physical probabilities as probabilities which are fixed
by a knowledge of *all* the relevant factors. The "all" is important. If we are uncertain as to some of them, we would
have our degrees of belief being a mixture of possible physical probabilities. We are thus led naturally to the following
characterization of the possible physical probability measures of which our epistemic probability measure is supposed to be a mixture:

I. *INVARIANCE:* A possible physical probability measure
should be invariant with respect to T.

II. *RESILIENCY:* A possible physical probability measure
should be such that it is not possible to
move to a "truer" physical probability by
conditionalizing on a further specification
of *projectible experimental factors.*

The second condition, *resiliency*, is the condition that we
have *all* the relevant factors built into our notion of possible
physical probability.

Of course, no non-degenerate probability space will be such
that the probability measure will be invariant under conditionalization on *any* set, so the question of *projectibility* is
vital. A specification of *projectible experimental factors* is
represented by a set in our probability space that is *invariant*

with respect to the transformation (technically: a set A such that the probability of the symmetric difference between A and $T^{-1}(A)$ has probability zero). The idea is that projectible factors should be invariant under the transformation which represents repetitions of the experiment.[38] Resiliency then becomes II': *There is no invariant set which the measure in question gives probability other than zero or one.* Conditioning on a set of measure one would leave the probability unchanged; conditioning on a set of measure zero is undefined. If a probability satisfies both I and II', I will say it is *objectively resilient* with respect to T. The desired representation theorem is then: Every probability *invariant* with respect to T has a unique representation as a mixture of probabilities that are *objectively resilient* with respect to T.

We also want our physical probabilities to have a connection with frequency. For a probability measure that is *objectively resilient* with respect to T, the transformation, T, is to be thought of as a repetition of the experiment with all the relevant factors fixed. For each point, ω, in the probability space, Ω, we can consider the sequence, ω, $T\omega$, $T(T\omega)$, ... $T^n\omega$ ..., and we can consider the relative frequency of any measurable set, A, in any finite segment of that sequence, and the limiting relative frequency in the sequence provided that it exists.

Call this sequence the (positive) *orbit* of ω. The nicest generalization of the law of large numbers that we could imagine here is that for any measurable set A, the limiting relative frequency of A in the orbit of ω exists and equals the physical probability of A almost everywhere (i.e., for every ω in Ω excepting a set of measure zero).

The theory that I have been hypothesizing already exists, although it is not usually viewed in this way. It is none other than the theory of measure-preserving transformations—the modern form of ergodic theory.[39] Where I said that the probability measure, P, is invariant with respect to T, the more usual terminology is that T is measure preserving with respect to P. Where I said that P is *objectively resilient* with respect to T, it is more common to say that T is *ergodic* (or metrically transitive or indecomposable) with respect to P.

The fantasized generalization of the law of large numbers is nothing other than Birkhoff's celebrated pointwise ergodic theorem[40] (or rather a special case thereof). The fantasized representation theorem is a version of the Kryloff-Bogoliouboff theorem.[41]

Actually, Birkhoff established the existence of the limiting relative frequency almost everywhere in general, when T is measure preserving with respect to P, but not necessarily ergodic with respect to P. If the transformation is, in addition, ergodic with respect to P, then the limiting relative frequency is almost everywhere constant and equal to the probability.[42]

In light of the representation theorem, this should be understood as follows: If the probability P is *invariant* with respect to T, then the limiting relative frequencies will almost surely converge to a probability measure P' which is one of the probability measures *objectively resilient* with respect to T. In terms of the interpretation we are pursuing here, let P be the probability measure representing your degrees of belief. Let T be a transformation which leaves your degrees of belief invariant. It determines your conception of a repetition of the same experiment and your notion of projectibility and your notion of *chance*. Then the limiting relative frequencies under repetition of the experiment will almost surely (with respect to your degrees of belief) converge to one of your chance distributions. *By virtue of a symmetry in your degrees of belief you must act as if you believe in objectively resilient chances to which you believe relative frequencies will converge.*

We characterized your objectively resilient "chance" probability measures as ones which were invariant under conditionalization on projectible predicates. We can show that these are the extreme points of the convex set of invariant measures. That is, we can show that a probability measure is objectively resilient if and only if it is (a) invariant and (b) cannot be represented as a non-trivial mixture:

$$P = (a/a + b)P_1 + (b/a + b)P_2 \qquad [a, b > 0; P_1 \neq P_2]$$

of distinct invariant measures.

Proof: One direction is trivial. If P is not objectively resilient, then by condition II there is a projectible property, A, such that $P(A) \neq 1$ & $P(A) \neq 0$. Then P can be written as a non-trivial mixture of invariant probability measures, i.e., the measures gotten by conditionalizing on A and on $\sim A$. For the other direction, notice that if P is a non-trivial average of P_1 and P_2, and P is objectively resilient, then P_1 and P_2 must be also, since under these assumptions P gives a set probability 0 only if P_1 and P_2 give it probability 0; likewise for probability one. Now suppose for *reductio* that P is objectively resilient and a non-trivial average of the invariant measures P_1 and P_2. Then, by the previous observation, P_1 and P_2 are also objectively resilient. By hypothesis, P_1 and P_2 are distinct, so there is a measurable set, A, to which they assign different values. By the ergodic theorem, the limiting relative frequency of A almost everywhere exists and is equal to $P_1(A)$, $P_2(A)$ and $P(A)$. This contradicts the assumption that $P_1(A) \neq P_2(A)$.

Historically, ergodic theory arose out of statistical mechanics. Birkhoff replaced Boltzmann's unworkable conception of ergodicity with the hypothesis of metric indecomposability. Here the transformation, T, is thought of as a time transformation specified by the dynamical law of the system. Then, taking M to be Lebesgue measure on phase space (suitably coordinatized), we have *invariance* with respect to T by Liouville's theorem. The question is whether one can prove that the Lebesgue measure restricted to constant energy hypersurfaces is objectively resilient (ergodic, metrically indecomposable) with respect to T. This is the version of the ergodic question that is relevant post-Birkhoff. Where the Kryloff-Bogoliouboff theorem applies we know that the Liouville measure on phase space is representable as a mixture of objectively resilient ergodic measures. We also know that each of these ergodic measures must concentrate probability one on some subset of a constant energy hypersurface, because the Liouville measure restricted to a given constant energy hypersurface is again an invariant measure. But the possibility is left open by the general theory that several ergodic measures each assign probability one to a different member of a partition of a given constant energy hypersurface. Whether this is so depends on the particular dynamical system in question. Proving the ergodic theorem for a given dynamical system requires proving that this is not so. This is an exceptionally difficult mathematical problem for the physical systems for which the theory was designed, and even for idealized approximations of them.[43] Although the mathematics of ergodic theory was born with the special concerns of statistical mechanics in mind it is congenial to the much more general interpretation that I have put on it.

The treatment of partial exchangeability for stochastic processes in the last section can be seen as a special case of the theory of measure-preserving transformations. Consider a stochastic process consisting of a doubly infinite sequence of random variables, $\ldots f_{-2}, f_{-1}, f_0, f_1, f_2 \ldots$, on a common probability space, S, and let Ω be the infinite product space whose elements consist of doubly infinite sequences of members of S, $\omega = (\omega_{-1}, \omega_0, \omega_1 \ldots)$. Let T be the *shift* transformation which takes $(\omega_{-1}, \omega_0, \omega_1, \ldots)$ to $(\omega_0, \omega_1, \omega_2 \ldots)$. Any statement about the random variables can be rephrased in terms of one of them and the shift transformation. To say that the shift is *measure preserving* or that the measure is *invariant* with respect to the shift is the same as saying that the stochastic process is *stationary*.

Suppose that the stochastic process is Bernoullian; that is, that the random variables are independent. Then the shift is ergodic with respect to the product measure on the product space, Ω. The Birkhoff ergodic theorem applied to this case gives the strong law of large numbers for Bernoulli sequences.[44] The Bernoullian measure is not the only sort of measure for which the shift transformation is ergodic. Certain Markov measures corresponding to certain Markov processes do as well.[45] So the Bernoullian measures are not the only extreme measures corresponding to the shift transformation. However, if, instead of the shift, we consider the group of transformations which take the sequence ω into another ω' just in case one can be gotten from the other by a finite permutation of its elements, the measures with respect to which that group of transformations is measure preserving are the exchangeable ones, and the objectively resilient probability measures are the independent ones.

The de Finetti analysis of exchangeable sequences as mixtures of independent ones is a special case of the theorems of ergodic theory. Freedman[46] uses the ergodic representation theorem as a tool to show that any stochastic process that is partially exchangeable with respect to the statistic consisting of the transition counts and the outcome of the first trial is a mixture of stationary Markov chains. In the course of this investigation he proves the more general theorem concerning partial exchangeability with respect to a statistic to which I referred in the previous section.

At a higher level of generality, the theory of measure-preserving transformations itself *is* the generalization of de Finetti's analysis. The theory of stationary stochastic processes is a special case. We need not confine ourselves to stochastic processes and to the shift transformation. Rather we can, under modest regularity conditions, consider an arbitrary probability space and an arbitrary measure-preserving transformation (or group of measure preserving transformations) which leave the probability invariant. This is quite a generalization.

The key element of the whole representation is the symmetry in one's subjective-probability measure, the transformation or group of transformations which leave it invariant. Does every subjective-probability distribution have some such symmetry? There is a trivial affirmative answer. The identity map is a measure-preserving transformation. If this is the only measure-preserving transformation for a person's subjective probability, then he will count as a repetition of the experiment only one with the same experimental conditions and the same experimental results. His chance distributions will each be concentrated on one point in his probability space. His conception of chance will be degenerate, with the chances all being zero or one. Most believers will have more generous symmetries in their degrees of belief, and will act as if they had a more interesting conception of chance.

We think of our group of transformations as varying those factors which are irrelevant to fixing the physical probabilities. Then the objectively resilient (ergodic) probability measures are intuitively probabilities conditional on the relevant experimental variables being fixed in a certain definite way. This intuition is correct in the following sense: *physical probability or chance* as a random variable is here probability conditional on the sub-sigma algebra of *projectible experimental factors* (invariant sets).[47] The chances you believe to be present in a given experiment (a point, ω,) are determined by the totality of the projectible experimental factors (invariant sets) which are present in that experiment (which have ω as a member). In this way, the invariant sets represent one's individuation of the chance setup.

We have now come almost full circle to the sort of picture given in section 1 of this chapter, but the account has gained in detail. There *chance* as a random variable was probability conditional on a partition; here that idea is given its straightforward generalization to probability conditional on a sub-sigma algebra. Furthermore, we can say something useful about this sub-sigma algebra. It is the sub-sigma algebra of invariant sets with respect to the transformation or group of transformations determining chance. To give a representation in terms of a person's degrees of belief about chance, we find the appropriate measure preserving transformations from his degrees of belief about experiments and outcomes.

Thus the question "When is it rational to have degrees of belief about chances, or to behave as if one does?" is reduced to the question of the rationality of degrees of belief about less mysterious entities. This is what I mean by a *pragmatic* reduction of the concept of chance.

Probabilistic Presuppositions of Induction

You can have your prior degrees of belief be in accordance with the probability calculus, conditionalize on your data and still refuse to learn from experience if your prior is concentrated on one extreme point. Or your state space for describing nature might be so pathological that the representation theorems fail because of failures in measurability. In this sense, induction has its probabilistic presuppositions.

Our conception of these presuppositions is profoundly transformed by the line of analysis initiated by de Finetti. I count the theory of measure-preserving transformations as part of this line of analysis. Invariance under a group of measure-preserving transformations is a natural generalization of partial exchangeability, even though it was not at first introduced with these concerns in mind.

The common theme of this line of analysis, at increasingly higher levels of generality, has been that the precondition for learning from experience is the adoption of an epistemic probability measure which is a nontrivial mixture of extremal measures. The effect of conditioning on a finite number of observations will, in general, be to remix the extremal measures with a different weighting function. As the number of observations goes to infinity, the weight almost surely concentrates on one of the extremal measures. We say that we learn what the *chances* (propensities, physical probabilities) are. In the special case of mixtures of independent sequences, this means that we have positive relevance of outcome types between trials; e.g., observation of a head makes it more likely that the next trial will come up heads. We do not have this type of learning from experience in general, and do not want it. As we approach concentration on the physical probabilities answering to the following Markov transition matrix:

	S_1	S_2
S_1	.1	.9
S_2	.9	.1

we want just the opposite. Learning from experience is best thought of as convergence to an extremal measure.

The ergodic theorem clarifies both the nature of the extremal measures and their connection with limiting relative frequency. Once we fasten on a relevant notion of repetition of an experiment by choice of a transformation which preserves our subjective probability measure, we find that the extremal measures are objectively resilient and that they satisfy the form of the law of large numbers with respect to repetitions of the experiment that finds expression in Birkhoff's ergodic theorem.

It is perhaps worthwhile underlining the differences between this analysis and customary applications of the strong law of large numbers for independent trials. In the first place, we are not assuming that *you*, the epistemic agent, *know* that the trials are independent or even that your degrees of belief exhibit any given symmetry. We assume only that your degrees of belief exhibit some symmetry or other, which is hardly any assumption at all. In the second place, there is the question of your proper attitude to the proof that there is convergence to a limiting relative frequency except for a set of points of measure zero. It is here inappropriate for you to ask the standard question, "Why should I believe that the real situation is not in that set of measure zero?" The measure in question *is* your degree of belief. You *do* believe that the real situation is not in that set, with degree of belief one.

We see how difficult it is to *not* behave inductively and to *not* believe in inductive success in the long run. We see how difficult it is to act as if one were *not* uncertain about chance. The interesting questions are not whether we do or should behave inductively, but about *how* we do or should behave inductively with respect to *what* conception of chance. These questions reduce to questions about the symmetries that we do or should have in our subjective degrees of belief.

4 A Bayesian Version of Causal Decision Theory

"Choice is not concerned with what has happened already: for example no one chooses to have sacked Troy; for neither does one deliberate about what has happened in the past, one deliberates about what still lies in the future and may happen or not; what has happened cannot be made not to have happened. Hence Agathon is right in saying:
   This alone is denied even to God
   The power to make what has been done undone.

Aristotle
Nichomachean Ethics VI, ii, 6

Chance is the ally of the prudent.

Euripides
Pirithous (Nauk fr. 598)

The idea that causal, modal, or counterfactual distinctions are central to the theory of rational decision is at least as old as Aristotle. According to the *Nichomachean Ethics*, we deliberate about factors which our actions may affect, not about factors which are already fixed.[1] This is an intuitive distinction, and we find something of the sort in various discussions of planning and rational decision: in the utilitarianism of Bentham and Mill, in Tinbergen's[2] distinction between data and target variables, and (arguably) in the distinction

---

This chapter in part overlaps and in part complements my "Causal Decision Theory," *Journal of Philosophy* 79, 11 (1982), 695–711.

between consequences and states of the world in the decision theory of L. J. Savage.[3]

Should such causal considerations be reflected in a general treatment of rational decision? If so, how? There have been several recent suggestions that the proper move is to explicitly incorporate subjunctive conditionals in one way or another into the model for rational decision.[4] On the face of it, these suggestions appear to constitute a challenge to the viewpoint of this book in two ways: first in calling for a revision of the foundations of the theory of subjective probability which forms the framework for our analyses and second in opening a metaphysical Pandora's box by introducing subjunctive conditionals. The overall purpose of this chapter is to show that things are not all that bad. A very general causal decision theory can be formulated without explicit introduction of subjunctive machinery in terms with which we are already familiar: *degree of belief* and *chance*. Indeed, in chapter 5 we will see how to turn the tables and use these ideas to give a general Bayesian treatment of subjunctive conditionals. And we will see that the accommodation of causal considerations is quite consistent with the framework of personal probability.

PRIMA FACIE COUNTEREXAMPLES
TO EVIDENTIAL DECISION THEORY

There is an alternative to the causal idea which would base deliberation on the *evidential* relation between the actions under consideration and various possible states of affairs. The evidential connection might be generated by various sorts of causal or non-causal beliefs: that the action causes the state of affairs, or that the state of affairs causes the action, or that there is an *analogy* between the two, and so forth. Under this evidential paradigm there is no presumption that the states of affairs which constitute payoffs are in any way consequences of the action. Here one evaluates actions as if they were *news items* about the world.[5] Evidence for good states of the world is good news; evidence for bad states of the world bad news. One deliberates so as to choose such actions as will constitute the best news.

In discussions of the foundations of subjective probability in this century, the difference between causal and evidential paradigms for deliberation has not always been treated with the explicitness that one might desire.[6] One exception is the precise formulation of the evidential paradigm in a very general setting in Richard Jeffrey's *The Logic of Decision*. There actions, consequences, and states of the world are all construed as propositions which are elements of one big Boolean algebra. Actions are there evaluated according to the degree of belief that the decision maker has for propositions conditional on the proposition that the action in question is taken. Taking the simple case where action A has positive degree of belief, and $[C_i]$ is a finite partition, we have:

Evidential Decision Theory:
VALUE $(A) = \Sigma_i$ DB(C_i given A) VALUE $(C_i$ & $A)$[7]

Can we find cases where evidential decision theory conflicts with the causal paradigm? It seems easy enough. Cases of spurious correlation are well known. Evidential relevance need not mirror causal relevance; the falling barometer does not cause the rain. So we might look for a case where action and payoff are correlated by being (probabilistic) effects of a common cause rather than by the action causing the payoff. Stalnaker[8] puts forward the following example: Suppose, contrary to our present best knowledge, that the correlation between smoking and lung cancer was due not to smoking's being a causative factor in the etiology of lung cancer; instead, that tendencies both to smoke and to develop lung cancer were effects of a common genetic cause.[9] Suppose that you *know* that the hypothesis is true, and that the evidential relevance of your smoking to your getting lung cancer is only by virtue of your smoking being evidence that you have the gene. Your smoking and your having cancer are probabilistically independent for you *conditional* on having the gene and *conditional* on not having it, although your smoking is, over all, positively relevant for you to your having cancer. Would it not then be foolish for you to decide not to smoke in order to lower the probability of your having cancer? Yet it appears that evidential decision theory makes just such a recommendation, in default of a way of taking into account the causal information we have built into the story.

Newcomb's paradox,[10] as usually conceived, is an infamous example of this type. A subject is about to be confronted with a decision problem, and has just taken an extensive psychological examination which predicts fairly well how subjects choose in such a situation. There are two boxes, one transparent and one opaque. The transparent box contains $1,000; the subject can see it. His choice is either to take only the contents of the opaque box or to take both boxes and get whatever is under the opaque box in addition to the $1,000. The experimenter, a wealthy eccentric, has put $1,000,000 under the opaque box if his test predicts that the subject will take only the opaque box; nothing under the opaque box if his test predicts that he will take both. Assume that about half of the people who take the test take one box and about half take two. Assume that the test is fairly reliable both for people who take the opaque box and for those who don't. The subject is told all this, and, being new to this sort of thing, his personal probabilities regarding his own trial are guided by the overall data. Assume for simplicity that dollars have constant utility for him. Indeed, to make the whole business so explicit as to preclude (I hope) misunderstanding, let his payoffs and personal conditional probabilities of the state given the act for this problem be as follows:

	Payoff	State $1,000,000 under	Nothing under
A C T	Take Opaque	$1,000,000	$0
	Take Both	$1,001,000	$1,000

	Degree of Belief	State $1,000,000 under opaque box	Nothing under opaque box
A C T	Take opaque	.6	.4
	Take Both	.4	.6

Evidential decision theory recommends taking only the opaque box, giving it a value of $600,000 as compared with a value of $401,000 for taking both boxes. But wouldn't our subject be irrational to take only the opaque box and forgo the $1,000 under the transparent box in the hopes that he will thus raise the probability of the million being under the opaque box? The million is either there or not, and his choice will not affect that.

Let's give this example one more twist. Suppose that both boxes are made of glass and that the opaque box is opaque only in that it is covered with a black velvet cloth. The subject is dithering over the correct choice, and finally the experimenter says: "All right. I'll offer you another option. You can lift the cloth, observe what's under the (previously) opaque box, and then choose as before. But I warn you that my reliability as a predictor holds up for subjects offered the third option."

What would you think of a subject who answered "Oh, no! You can't fool me. I won't look. I'll just take the box with the cloth over it"? Evidential decision theory can recommend just such a course of action. The subject knows that if he peeks, no matter whether he observes the million under the opaque box or not, he will then take both boxes since he prefers a million and a thousand to a thousand, and a thousand to nothing. Then, with proper elaboration of the story, he may take the decision to peek as evidence that there is nothing under the opaque box whereas the decision to take only the opaque box is good evidence that it contains the million. But peeking won't change what's under the boxes.

The evidential relevance in the two foregoing examples was generated by a belief that action and state of the world are effects of a common cause. There are many familiar examples of this type, but one shouldn't think that this is the only sort of situation in which evidential relevance fails to mirror causal relevance in the appropriate way. Evidential relevance might be set up by belief in all sorts of causal networks, but it might also be set up by reasoning by *analogy*. With proper elaboration,[11] the Prisoner's Dilemma paradox constitutes just such an example. Two confederates in crime are taken prisoner. They are kept in separate cells without possibility of communication, and let us suppose that there is no opportunity for later retaliation. If one confesses and the other doesn't, the one who confesses gets off free while the other gets a very long prison sentence. If both confess, they get long prison terms. If neither confesses the state has only enough evidence to put them away for a short time. Suppose that each prisoner is initially unsure as to what he will do, but each believes that he is really very much like the other. Then for each prisoner, what he decides to do may be evidence for what the other prisoner will decide to do. You can fill in the details so that evidential decision theory recommends to each prisoner that he confess. But it is hard to believe that the foundations for mutual cooperation can be laid that easily. What action one prisoner chooses will not influence what the other does.

These are the basic sorts of *prima facie* counterexamples to evidential decision theory that have been put forward. Evidential decision theory appears to recommend the wrong answer. How should we formulate a general theory of decision which embodies the competing causal paradigm?

CAUSAL DECISION THEORY

Stalnaker's 1972 suggestion[12] was to reformulate expected utility by replacing conditional probability with the probability of a subjunctive conditional:

Σ_i DB(If A were taken, Consequence C would ensue)
Utility (C_i)

This proposal is developed by Gibbard and Harper[13], and generalized to conditionals with chance consequents by Lewis.[14]

We can, however, formulate causal decision theory in terms that we have already discussed: in terms of the interaction between degree of belief and chance. This formulation will owe more to Savage than to Stalnaker, although given the Bayesian theory of conditionals to be developed in the next chapter, it will be seen to be compatible with the approach that uses subjunctive conditionals.

Life is a continual gamble, with the chances of payoffs being determined partly by background factors over which we have no control and of which we have only imperfect knowledge and partly by our choice of action (which is why "Chance is the ally of the prudent" to the extent that she is). We will distinguish these two determinants of the chances of payoffs because of their different roles in practical reasoning. The causal background is not an object of *choice*: No one chooses to have sacked Troy, to have been born with the smoking-cancer gene, to have been predicted to have taken one box. Acts are, on the other hand, the immediate objects of choice. Their value *qua* object of choice will depend on the chances of payoffs or *consequences* which they, together with the background factors determine. We will then, like Savage, distinguish three categories: maximal constellations of background factors or *states of the world*, *acts*, and *consequences*. Acts and states of the world will jointly determine unconditional chances of consequences. (We could put the same point in a slightly different way by saying that the states alone determine *conditional chances* of the consequences conditional on the acts. The conditional chances cannot be affected by our choice of act.) We could, if we so desired, think of acts as functions from states to unconditional chance distributions over consequences; there is such a function for every act. We could, if we so desired, think of states of the world as *functions* from acts to chance distributions over consequences. But I prefer to think of States, Acts, and Consequences as all primitive.

These distinctions are clearly exemplified in the following decision situation: You are in a hall with a quarter to play in one of a row of slot machines. The machines may have quite different chances of payoffs associated with them. You may know something about the machines, perhaps you have observed a day's play on them, but you do not know enough of the internal workings and settings to determine the chances of payoffs for each machine. Your *act* is to play machine one, or machine two or ... The *state of the world* is constituted by the internal workings and settings which determine the chances of payoffs, if played, of all the machines. The *con-*

sequences are the payoffs. Alternatively, there might be only one machine, with your act consisting in setting a dial, or some other input.

We define the utility *qua* Act of an action in two stages. Relative to a state of the world, K, the act A has an *objective expected utility* as a gamble over consequences:

$$U_K(A) = \Sigma_i \; \text{CHANCE}_{K,A}(C_i)\text{UTILITY}_K(A \; \& \; C_i)^{15}$$

If one knows the state of the world, then one should choose the act with greatest objective expected utility. But if one is uncertain as to the state of the world, one does not know which act has the greatest objective expected utility, and can do no better than to go by its subjective expectation:

$$U(A) = \Sigma_j \text{DEGREE OF BELIEF } (K_j)\Sigma_i \text{CHANCE}_{K,A}(C_i)$$
$$U_K(A \; \& \; C_i)$$

We follow Savage in taking an unconditional expectation rather than one conditional on the action (using $DB[K]$ rather than $DB[K$ given $A]$) because, by definition, the acts do not influence the states.[16]

Assuming, as we are here for the sake of simplicity, that there are just a finite number of states, acts, and consequences, and each conjunction of state and acts has some positive prior degree of belief, we can rewrite CHANCE as degree of belief conditional on the factors which the decision maker takes as determining chance:

$$\text{CHANCE}_{K,A}(C) = DB(C \text{ given } A \; \& \; K)$$

This allows us to write:

$$U(A) = \Sigma_j \; DB(K_j) \; \Sigma_i DB(C_i \text{ given } A \; \& \; K_j) \; U(A \; \& \; K_j \; \& \; C_i)$$

as I have it in *Causal Necessity*.[17] In more complicated cases we will have the expectations as integrals and the relation of chance and degree of belief determined by the representation theorems discussed in chapter 3.

The essential idea of the version of causal decision theory under consideration is, then, that *preference for action* should go by an unconditional degree-of-belief expectation of a chance expectation of consequences; the chances being jointly determined by the acts and the states of the world, and the acts having no influence on the states of the world. Let us see how this theory handles the *prima facie* counterexamples to evidential decision theory.

Consider Newcomb's paradox. The states are: (K_1) $1,000,000 is under the opaque box and $1,000 is under the transparent box and (K_2) Nothing is under the opaque box and $1,000 is under the transparent box. The acts are: (A_1) Take only the opaque box and (A_2) Take both. The consequences are: (C_{11}) Get $1,000,000; (C_{12}) Get $1,001,000; $C_{21})$ Get nothing; (C_{22}) Get $1,000. In this particular example the chances are degenerate; they are either zero or one. The chance of getting a million if you take only one box and there is a million under it is one. With the way that I have subscripted the consequences, Chance$_{ij}$ (Consequence$_{ij}$) = 1. For each state of the world, the *objective expected utility relative to that state* of taking both boxes exceeds that of taking the opaque box by $1,000: $U_{K1}(A_2)$ = $1,001,000 while $U_{K1}(A_1)$ = 1,000,000; $U_{K2})$ = $1,000 while $U_{K2}(A_2)$ = 0. Consequently the subjective expectation of objective expected utility for (A_2) will exceed that for (A_1) by $1,000. Causal decision theory unambiguously recommends taking two boxes.[18] In the smoking–lung cancer example, and in the Prisoner's Dilemma case a realistic filling out of the examples will be indeterministic, and chance will be non-degenerate. Causal decision theory will recommend smoking and confessing respectively, in contrast to evidential decision theory.

Causal decision theory may be expected to often differ from evidential decision theory in game-theoretic situations, where the chances of my payoffs may be jointly determined by (1) pre-existing factors over which I have no influence, and (2) factors which I can influence by my actions, in particular, by my opponent's actions.

If the *prima facie* counterexamples to evidential decision theory are genuine counterexamples, then they can be met by the kind of causal decision theory given. It is not necessary to import all of the complexities of the semantics of subjunctive conditionals into the theory of rational decision

in order to give causal considerations their due. Nevertheless, the ideas used here are closely connected with theories
of subjunctive conditionals, as will be made clear in the next
chapter.

But it remains to consider further whether the *prima facie*
counterexamples are genuine counterexamples. For evidential decision theory does have *some* sensitivity to causal considerations. We now ask how far that sensitivity can be pushed.

TICKLES AND METATICKLES

In the example of smoking and lung cancer, suppose that the
smoking-cancer gene promoted smoking by causing a certain
phenomenologically identifiable tickle in the lungs and that
the agent knows this and knows how to identify the tickle
in his own case. Then, even if he uses evidential decision
theory he will smoke. (we pretend for the sake of the example that smoking is otherwise harmless and pleasurable)
since he *knows* whether he has the tickle or not, and thereby
knows the state of the world. *For an agent who knows the
state of the world, causal and evidential decision theory
coincide.*

Let us weaken the example slightly. Suppose now that a
few people without the gene have the tickle or something
mistakable for it, and a few without the gene don't, but that
the presence of the tickle indicates presence of the gene as
well as the decision to smoke or not does, and suppose that
the agent knows all this and it is reflected in his degrees of
belief as follows: In his degrees of belief, smoking is independent of having the gene *conditional* on having the tickle,
and *conditional* on not having the tickle. Then, since he
knows whether he has the tickle or not, *his* smoking is in *his*
degrees of belief probabilistically independent of *his* having
the gene. Then the putative confrontation between causal
and evidential decision theory again vanishes, for when the
states are evidentially independent of the actions, causal and
evidential decision theory coincide.

There is no doubt that the counterpart of the tickle often

exists, and that one can retell the stories that constitute *prima facie* counterexamples to evidential decision theory in a way that introduces such a counterpart. Such retellings are not counterexamples to evidential decision theory. Could we argue that there is *always* a counterpart of the tickle, so that evidential decision theory would, on closer analysis, *always* coincide with causal decision theory? If so, the challenge of the causal examples could be met in a simpler way than by the formulation of causal decision theory that I gave in the last section; evidential decision theory would be all right as it stands. But how can we guarantee for the decision maker the existence of the counterpart of the tickle?

What is crucial is that the decision maker must know whether the tickle is present, and that for him the acts are evidentially independent of the states *conditional* on knowledge about the tickle. One might argue that common causes of acts and states or causal bases of analogies setting up evidential relevance between acts and states can only operate by influencing the agent's beliefs and desires; at least if he is a rational agent. One might then suspect that if the agent knew his own mind, he would know as much (or almost as much) about himself as the act will tell him; his degrees of belief would approximate independence of acts and states; for him, evidential decision theory would approximate causal decision theory. So one might attempt to develop a theory of the *Sophisticated Decision Maker* wherein sophistication is characterized stringently enough in terms of self-knowledge and causal reasoning that for such decision makers the two paradigms are in approximate agreement. A subtle and insightful theory of the sophisticated decision maker has recently been developed along these lines by Ellery Eells.[19] Eells' decision maker is sophisticated indeed. He not only is rational but also knows that he is rational. He has degrees of belief about his degrees of belief and desires, and about acts and consequences conditional on his degrees of belief and desires. In return for this sophistication, Eells's decision maker has a greatly enhanced sensitivity to causal considerations *via* what we might call "metatickles."

There is a generic problem with this sort of approach. The

theory must walk a tightrope between too much self-knowledge and too little. If the decision maker has too little self-knowledge, there is room for the wrong kind of evidential relevance of act to state to creep in. If the individual has too much self-knowledge, then he already knows what he will do and there is no decision problem (i.e., his prior probability that he will choose a certain act is one.) Eells accepts this and ventures out on the tightrope.

A natural way to try to avoid the tightrope (although not one that should be attributed to Eells) is to adopt a diachronic version of the metatickle defense. That is, one could argue that *as the decision maker deliberates*, he learns more and more about himself until, *at the moment of choice*, he knows as much about himself as the choice of act will tell him. Then, plausibly, evidential independence is approached during deliberation guaranteeing the (approximate?) agreement of causal and evidential decision theory, and the decision problem does not collapse until it should— at the moment of choice.[20]

In *The Logic of Decision* (2nd ed.), Jeffrey suggests a related but distinct line of defense for evidential decision theory. This consists in a *hypothetical* version of the metatickle defense:

> A ratifiable decision is a decision to perform an act of maximum estimated desirability relative to the probability matrix the agent thinks he would have if he finally decided to perform the act.[21]

The idea is that if there is a unique ratifiable act, the rational choice is to choose that one. The unique ratifiable act may not correspond to the act with current maximum expected utility (e.g., in Newcomb's paradox) because metatickles are factored into the hypothetical final probability that the agent thinks he would have at the moment of decision. Suppose that agent believes that were he to choose one box, at the moment of choice he would be sure that the million is stashed *no matter what*, and therefore that taking two boxes would have an expected utility of $1,001,000. Taking one box is therefore not ratifiable for him. Taking two boxes is ratifiable for him, supposing that he believes that at the moment of choice of two boxes he would be sure that there is no million stashed no matter what.

We have three variations of the theme that metatickles can make evidential decision theory sensitive to causal considerations: (I) the Eells version, in which metatickles and expected utility maximization are postulated at the moment of decision; (II) the diachronic metatickle defense, which retains expected utility maximization but has metatickles evolve during deliberation; and (III) the hypothetical metatickle defense of Jeffrey, which replaces expected utility maximization with the rule of ratifiability.

For decision makers sophisticated enough to use them, each of these lines shows how the basic structure of evidential decision theory can respond in some degree to causal considerations. But it remains to be seen, under each of these proposals, whether the increase in sensitivity to causal considerations is sufficient to secure the virtues of causal decision theory.

DELIBERATION, PROBABILITY DYNAMICS

How does probability evolve as we deliberate about which act to perform? Deliberation about our big decision can be thought of as comprised of a series of infinitesimal decisions to "lean a little bit more this way or that." Following this line of thought, we consider a model of deliberation wherein the rate of flow of probability between actions under consideration is a function of the difference in their expected utilities.

Even the simplest cases of such models are not without interest. Suppose that there are just two alternative acts: A_1, A_2; and that the time derivative of the probability of an act is proportional to the increment in expected utility of it over its competitor:

$$d\, DB(A_1) \propto \text{Expected Utility } A_1 - \text{Expected Utility } A_2$$

until such time as the probability of one of the acts hits one (which ends the deliberation).[22]

Within the model, we can study the trajectory of $DB(A)$ relative to different senses of expected utility. In particular, we can compare the effect on certain decision problems of taking expected utility to be either epistemic conditional expected utility or the epistemic expectation of a chance expectation used in causal decision theory.

Let us first consider evidential decision theory, whereby:

Expected Utility $= \Sigma_i\, DB(C_i/A)V(C_i\ \&\ A)$

Suppose that the utilities, $V(C_i\ \&\ A)$, remain constant over time. Then the salient question is how the conditional degrees of belief $DB(C_i\ \&\ A)$ change over time. In many decision situations it is plausible to say that they don't. These are situations in which probability evolves, as Jeffrey would say,[23] by "probability kinematics" on the acts. In such cases, deliberation is straightforward and uninteresting, as in figure 1.

There are, however, situations in which the decision maker might take his own deliberations as supplying information which affects the epistemic probabilities of the consequence conditional on the act. Under the hypothesis that Eellsian metatickles develop during deliberation, Newcomb's paradox and related forms of Prisoner's Dilemma are examples. Let us investigate the structure of deliberation in such examples.

Consider Newcomb's paradox, letting A_1 be the act of taking the one opaque box and A_2 being the act of taking both

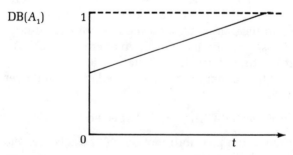

Figure 1

boxes. Suppose that deliberation begins with the decision maker sitting on the fence: $DB(A_1) = DB(A_2) = \frac{1}{2}$. Evidential expected utility favors A_1, so deliberation starts moving toward the one-box decision (see figure 2).

But, under the hypothesis of the development of Eellsian metatickles, the decision maker becomes more and more sure on the evidence of his own deliberations that the million is stashed under the opaque box (M) *no matter what*. That is as $DB(A_1)$ approaches one, $DB(M/A_2)$ approaches the initially high value of $DB(M/A_1)$. We know that if the decision maker is sure that the million is stashed *no matter what*, taking two boxes has a greater expected utility than taking one box by $1,000. Assuming that metatickles develop continuously (i.e. that $|DB(M/A_1) - DB(M/A_2)|$ is a continuous function of $DB(A_1)$), the difference in expected utility must also develop continuously, so (by the mean value theorem) there must be a point short of one where second thoughts crowd in on the decision maker, where the difference in expected utility between the acts and thus the time derivative of $DB(A_1)$ is zero (see figure 3). So, assuming the effectiveness of the metatickles, evidential decision theory avoids closing deliberation with the one-box solution.

Let us also assume equal effectiveness for metatickles as $DB(A_1)$ approaches zero. As the decision maker becomes more and more sure in his deliberations that he will take both boxes, his knowledge of his deliberations tends to screen off

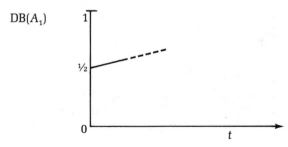

Figure 2

the act itself, and he becomes more and more sure that the million is stashed regardless of the act. That is, as $DB(A_1)$ approaches zero, $DB(M/A_1)$ and $DB(M/A_2)$ approach the initial value of $DB(M/A_2)$. This means that there is some critical region where $DB(A_1)$ is close to zero where the value of A_2 is again greater than that of A_1, so that if the trajectory of $DB(A_1)$ enters that region it will hit zero and end deliberation with a two-box act (see figure 4).

So far, so good. Metatickles allow the decision maker not only to avoid closing deliberation with a one-box solution but also to recognize the two-box solution as correct provided he gets close enough to taking it. But not every decision maker will get that close. The decision maker who started at $DB(A_1) = \frac{1}{2}$ is a case in point. His trajectory looks like that in figure 5. His deliberation remains stuck; he is almost

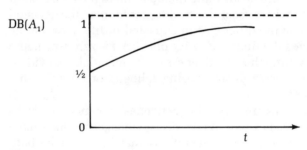

Figure 3

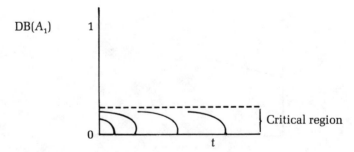

Figure 4

sure that one box is the way to go, but never free of those nagging Eellsian doubts. Trajectories in the whole space look roughly like those in figure 6.

We could set up oscillations by giving $Pr(A_1)$ some inertia and damp them by letting him be less confident in the efficacy of his self-knowledge-as-symptom the second time around, but these moves toward greater realism would only make things worse as far as the metatickle defense goes.

Now consider the same problem from the standpoint of causal decision theory:

Expected value $(A) =$
$$\Sigma_i \, DB(K_i) \, \Sigma_j DB(C_j/A \, \& \, K_i) \, V(C_j \, \& \, A \, \& \, K_i)$$

If $DB(K_i)$ and $DB(C_j/A \, \& \, K_i)$ and the values $V(C_j \, \& \, A \, \& \, K_i)$ remain constant, we get straight line deliberation. $DB(K_i/A)$

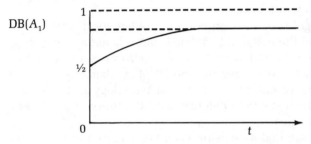

Figure 5

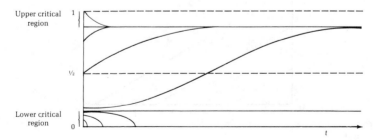

Figure 6

doesn't come into it. But in Newcomb-type situations the value of the K_i's may change during deliberation since the evolution of $DB(A_1)$ may be a symptom of the state of the world. (In Newcomb's problem, the relevant K_i's can be taken to be M and $-M$: the crucial background factors are whether the million has been stashed or not.) No matter, for in Newcomb's problem the difference in expected value between A_2 and A_1 is constant no matter how $DB(M)$ varies. Deliberation leads straight to the two-box solution (see figure 7). Examination of the diachronic version of the metatickle defense discloses difficulties that are not apparent if one focuses on the final choices. Here there was, indeed, only one equilibrium decision: *take both boxes*. But many evidential decision theorists would arrive at an equilibrium *indecision*, whereas causal decision theorists would not.

A Problem for Eells

The foregoing discussion poses a problem for the diachronic version of the metatickle defense, but it is not a direct counterexample to Eells's version or to Jeffrey's Ratificationism, since neither endorses the model of deliberation at issue. However, we can uncover related pathology in Eells's version of the metatickle defense, with the introduction of random strategies.

Let us say that a decision is an *Eells equilibrium* if, at the moment of truth, the agent making it considers it to be opti-

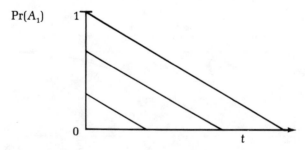

Figure 7

mal. I take it to be the essential point of Eells's position that a rational agent can only choose an Eells-equilibrium act. His defense of epistemic conditional expected utility in the original Newcomb problem is that given effective meta-tickles there is only one Eells-equilibrium decision, i.e., take both boxes. In some decision problems there are no Eells equilibria, but in many of such cases[24] the introduction of random (or mixed) strategies assures the existence of an Eells-equilibrium decision.

Let us consider the question of Eells equilibria for New-comb's problem with random strategies and metatickles. The decision maker delegates his choice of boxes to his home computer, which chooses between A_1(take the opaque box) and A_2(take both) with respective probabilities of x and $1 - $ x. The decision maker's problem is then which value of x to choose. Let us suppose that the decision maker believes that the predictor's accuracy with regard to the prediction of A_1 or A_2 holds up conditional on each choice of x. He believes not only that the predictor knows him inside and out but also that the predictor knows his Kaypro (and his random-choice program) inside and out. (The choice looks random to the decision maker, but he believes that it does not look random to the predictor.) The decision maker is initially un-certain of what value of x he will choose.

Let us also assume the presence of *metatickles*. Given the story, we can plausibly assume that they work as follows. At the time that the decision maker selects the value of x, he has a probability, $[Pr_x]$, influenced by the value of x that he has selected. The closer x is to one, the surer the agent is when he punches it into the computer that the million is stashed *no matter what* (i.e., conditional on each value of x being the one chosen). Likewise, if he were to choose a value of x very near zero, he would be very sure that nothing was stashed *no matter what*. At x = 0 and x = 1 the metatickles screen off perfectly; probability of stash is independent of act in Pr_0 and Pr_1. At x = ½ there is no screening off, because of the decision maker's uncertainty about whether he will end up with A_1 or A_2. The degree of screening off by meta-tickles increases continuously as x approaches one or zero.

Now I claim that in the problem as presented there are *two* Eells equilibria. One is at x = 0, the choice of two boxes for sure. The other, by a continuity argument similar to the one used in the last section, is somewhere between x = ½ and x = 1. The second equilibrium point does not exist for causal decision theory and is, I claim, an *incorrect decision*.

Here is a realization of the example with numerical values. The player starts out with an initial probability [Pr_i] which gets bent by metatickles into a final probability [Pr_x] when the player chooses the random strategy that gives probability x of taking one box. In the initial probability distribution, the player thinks that the predictor will do well no matter what. For simplicity:

$$Pr_i[\text{STASH/1 Box \& } Pr_x(1 \text{ box}) = \alpha] = 1 \text{ (for all values of } \alpha)$$

$$Pr_i[\text{STASH/2 Box \& } Pr_x(1 \text{ box}) = \alpha] = 0 \text{ (for all values of } \alpha)$$

where "STASH" is the proposition that the million is stashed under the opaque box.

If the player chooses the random strategy that makes 1 box and 2 box equiprobable, then there is no reason for there to be any screening off by metatickles:

$$[Pr_{x = ½}] = [Pr_i]$$

On the other hand, the choice of the random strategy with x = 1 is tantamount to the choice of the pure strategy of taking one box, and the metatickles should screen off in just the way hypothesized for that pure strategy. The player will be sure that the million is stashed no matter what:

$$Pr_{x=1}[\text{STASH/1 Box \& } Pr_y(1 \text{ box}) = \alpha] = 1 \text{ (for all values of } \alpha)$$

$$Pr_{x=1}[\text{STASH/2 Box \& } Pr_y(1 \text{ box}) = \alpha] = 1 \text{ (for all values of } \alpha)$$

Likewise, on the choice of $x = 0$ the player has arrived at a probability distribution which gives probability zero to STASH conditional on his adopting any mixed strategy eventuating in any final selection:

$Pr_{x=0}[\text{STASH}/1 \text{ box} \ \& \ Pr(1 \text{ box}) = \alpha] = 0$ (for all values of α)

$Pr_{x=0}[\text{STASH}/2 \text{ box} \ \& \ Pr(1 \text{ box}) = \alpha] = 0$ (for all values of α)

In between these extremes, metatickles screen off more as we approach $x = 1$ and $x = 0$, less as we approach $x = \frac{1}{2}$:

For $x \geqslant \frac{1}{2}$:

$Pr_x[\text{STASH}/1 \text{ box} \ \& \ Pr(1 \text{ box}) = \alpha] = 1$ (for all values of α)

$Pr_x[\text{STASH}/2 \text{ box} \ \& \ Pr(2 \text{ box}) = \alpha] = 2x - 1$ (for all values of α)

For $x \leqslant \frac{1}{2}$:

$Pr_x[\text{STASH}/1 \text{ box} \ \& \ Pr(1 \text{ box}) = \alpha] = 2x$ (for all values of α)

$Pr_x[\text{STASH}/2 \text{ box} \ \& \ Pr(2 \text{ box}) = \alpha] = 0$ (for all values of α)

Now if a player chooses a random strategy which gives probability x of taking one box, he has a corresponding probability which gives an epistemic conditional expected utility for not only the random strategy he chose, but for each random strategy corresponding to a probability, α, for choosing one box. We denote this expected utility by:

$EU_x(\alpha)$

Let the amount that may be stashed under the opaque box be M and that under the transparent box be T. Then in our example, for values of x greater than or equal to $\frac{1}{2}$, we have:

$EU_x(\alpha) = \alpha M + (1 - \alpha) T + (1 - \alpha)(2x - 1) M$

An Eells equilibrium is a value of x for which:

$EU_x(x) > EU_x(\alpha)$ for all α

For our example, we have an Eells equilibrium at $x = 1 - (T/2M)$. Taking T as \$1,000 and M as \$1,000,000 as in the original story, we have an Eells equilibrium at $x = .9995$. [At $x = .9995$, $EU_x(x) = EU_x(\alpha) = \$1,000,000$ (for all α).] There is also an Eells equilibrium at $x = 0$. At $x = 0$, $EU_x(x) = \$1,000$ and $EU_x(\alpha) = \$1,000(1 - \alpha)$.

Presumably a rational Eellsian agent could choose either of them, and would certainly not be irrational in choosing that with the greater expected utility from its own standpoint. But choice of a mixed strategy at $x = .9995$ by a decision maker whose subjective probabilities are as postulated in the example is as irrational by the lights of causal decision theory as the choice of the pure strategy of taking one box.

A PROBLEM FOR RATIFIABILITY

Neither of the foregoing two sections gives a direct counterexample to ratifiability. The section on probability dynamics is not relevant because Ratificationism specifies a "look and leap" model of deliberation quite different from the continuous expected utility maximization model presented there. The decision maker is supposed to look at the hypothetical posterior probability distributions that he thinks he would have upon choosing various acts, [pr_j] corresponding to act j, and then leap to the performance of a ratifiable act, i.e., an act, A_k, which looks optimal when evaluated with respect to [pr_k]. If the decision maker is *right* about which posterior distributions he would have upon doing given acts, then for him the ratifiable acts are the Eells equilibrium acts.

In Newcomb's problem there is a unique ratifiable act, *take both boxes*, so evidential decision theory as modified by the doctrine of Ratificationism agrees here with causal decision theory as to the correct choice of act. If there is no ratifiable act, or more than one, then Ratificationism, as set forth by Jeffrey, makes no recommendation other than that the decision maker reassess his beliefs and desires. So the example of Newcomb's problem with random strategies with two

equilibrium decisions is not directly relevant to Ratificationism either.

Here is a problem that is. You are to choose one of three
shells [A_1, A_2, A_3], and will receive what is under it. No
mixed acts are allowed. (If you attempt to randomize, even
mentally, the attempt will be detected and you will be shot.)
A very good predictor has predicted your choice. If he predicted A_1 he put 10¢ under shell one and nothing under the
others. If he predicted A_2, he put $10 under shell two and
$100 under shell three. If he predicted A_3, he put $20 under
shell three and $200 under shell two. The three possible
states of the world just described are K_1, K_2, K_3 respectively.
Let us assume that when presented with the problem, you
judge the three states equiprobable, $Pr_i(K_j) = ⅓$. Let us also
assume, for simplicity, that the predictor is initially thought
to be perfect, $Pr_i(K_j/A_j) = 1$. This assumption is in no way
essential.

You have hypothetical posteriors which represent what
you think your probabilities will be at the moment of taking
one of the actions (pr_1; pr_2; pr_3). We grant here, for the sake
of argument, the presence of metatickles that are perfectly
effective in indicating the state of the world:

$pr_1(K_1/A_j) = 1$ for all values of j

$pr_2(K_2/A_j) = 1$ for all values of j

$pr_3(K_3/A_j) = 1$ for all values of j

In the problem just given, there is a unique ratifiable act,
A_1. According to the rule of ratifiability, one should choose
A_1. But A_1 has the least prior expected utility of the three
acts according to both causal and evidential decision theory:

Expected Utility	Evidential	Causal
A_1	10¢	3⅓¢
A_2	$10	⅓($10) + ⅓($200)
A_3	$20	⅓($20) + ⅓($100)

Both causal and evidential decision theorists who deliberate by continuous probability maximization may have trouble with this problem, hanging up between A_2 and A_3. Followers of the rule of ratifiability do not have this difficulty. They "look and leap." *But they leap to the wrong decision.* "Look and leap" deliberation is attractive for this sort of problem; it is just the sort of deliberation that a rule-utilitarian analysis of deliberation would recommend here. But if you are going to look and leap, and you believe that your choice of action will not influence the state of the world, you should leap to A_2.

METATICKLES ASSESSED

If the metatickle defenses of evidential expected utility theory succeeded, then we would need not worry about fitting causal decision theory into an empiricist framework. But they do not succeed. They show that evidential decision theory is sometimes sensitive to causal considerations, and they raise interesting theoretical questions about deliberation. But they fail to show that evidential decision theory is adequate to the concerns of causal decision theory.

Tickles and metatickles *may just not give us enough information about the true state of the world*, as in Newcomb's problem with random strategies. This problem is brought home to Ratificationism in a version of Prisoner's Dilemma due to van Fraassen, which Jeffrey reports in the second edition of *The Logic of Decision*. It is the reason that Jeffrey concludes, in the end, that ratifiability fails to capture choiceworthiness.

Even where metatickles at the moment of decision give us perfect information about the state of nature, evidential decision theory is not equivalent to causal decision theory with respect to the *structure of deliberation*. This is true for both continuous expected utility models of deliberation, and "look and leap" models of deliberation. In the first case, the evidential decision theorist may never get to the point of decision but rather be stuck at an equilibrium indecision. "Look and leap" deliberation avoids indecision, but ratificationists may leap to the wrong decision where causal decision theorists leap to the right one.

Furthermore, it should be noticed that as the metatickle defenses become more sophisticated, they move in as much conceptual machinery as is needed for the Bayesian version of causal decision theory put forward in this chapter. If we can consider hypothetical posteriors that we think we would have at the moment of truth in the presence of effective metatickles, why can't we consider the hypothetical probabilities that we think we would have if we knew the state of the world, K, calculate an "objective expectation" for each, and take the epistemic expectation of these objective expectations? That is all we need for causal decision theory.

THE LONG RUN

Why should your preferences go by expected utility? The answer we gave in chapter 2 was that for reasonable preference orderings, embeddible in reasonable preference orderings over a rich set of alternatives, we can prove a *representation theorem* which says that we can supply utilities and probabilities such that the preferences go by expected utility.

There is another sort of rationale, which was invoked by early probability theorists with regard to games of chance. That is the argument from the long run. In a long run of independent trials of a game of chance, the argument goes, the average winnings per trial will almost certainly converge to the expected winnings on a single trial. The principle of expected value is justified by the law of large numbers.

There are familiar objections against the pragmatic relevance of the long run which I will not discuss here. Rather, tabling these objections, I want to ask how the argument cuts with respect to evidential versus causal decision theory. I have heard the idea expressed that long-run considerations favor evidential decision theory over causal decision theory. This idea will be seen to rest on a *fallacy*.

An argument from the long run must rest on some limit

theorem: some generalization of the law of large numbers. Let us recall the discussions of chapter 3 about how such generalizations work when we have an interaction of degree of belief and chance. Remember the example of the biased coin. The agent has degree of belief of ½ in each of two hypotheses: (1) that the chance of heads is ⅔, and (2) that the chance of heads is ⅓. His degree of belief that heads will come up in a given single toss is ½. The relevant form of the law of large numbers shows that he has degree of belief one that in an infinite sequence of independent trials, the relative frequency will converge to either ⅓ or ⅔. He does not think that the relative frequency will converge to the single-case degree of belief of ½; to conclude that would be the *fallacy* of invoking a convergence theorem whose conditions of application are not fulfilled in this case. The example generalizes. Given the general treatment of chance *via* ergodic theory in chapter 3, in the typical situation in which we are uncertain about what the chances are, we believe with degree of belief one that the relative frequencies in an infinite sequence of repetitions of the experiment will converge to one of the possible chance distributions. In special cases of games of chance where we are certain as to what the chances are, we can believe with probability one that the long-run relative frequencies will converge to the chances (which in these special situations are equal to the single-case degree of belief). But in the more general case where we are uncertain about the chances, we must rely on the generalized limit theorems.

What do these theorems tell us about the limiting empirical average of a random variable? They tell us that it will, with degree of belief one, converge to the chance expectation in one of the possible chance distributions. For instance, in the example of an infinite sequence of objectively independent trials of the biased coin, suppose that we have a random variable that takes on the value $1 if the coin comes up heads and zero otherwise. Then the agent's degree of belief will be one that the limiting empirical average in the infinite sequence will converge to either $⅔ or $⅓. Taking the value of the random variable to indicate the payoff of bet, the average winnings per trial will almost certainly converge to the true *chance* expectation of winnings on a single trial.

Then if the long-run argument justifies anything, what it justifies is our definition of the *objective expected utility* of an act A at state of the world K as $U_K(A) = \Sigma_i$ $\text{CHANCE}_{K,A}(C_i)\text{UTILITY}(C_i)$. If the state of the world is such that the coin is biased two to one toward heads, then the objective expected utility of a bet on a single trial is almost surely equal to the limiting average winnings on a sequence of objectively independent trials.

We see even more than this from this sort of Bayesian analysis. Suppose that we have two random variables in the biased coin case: B_1 takes on the value $1 if the coin comes up heads and $0 if it comes up tails; B_2 takes on the value $1.01 if the coin comes up heads and $0.01 if it comes up tails.

Our decision maker will believe with degree of belief one that the limiting relative frequency of heads on an infinite sequence of objectively independent flips of this coin will be either ⅔ or ⅓ according to which hypothesis about the chances is correct; he believes with degree of belief one that the limiting average winnings per trial for B_1 in such a sequence will be either $⅔ or $⅓ and for B_2 $⅔ + ⅔ cents or $⅓ + ⅓, respectively. *He therefore believes with degree of belief one that the limiting average winnings per trial in an infinite number of objectively independent trials for bet B_2 will be greater than that for bet B_1.*

Consider Newcomb's paradox. The role of chance is somewhat masked by the deterministic nature of the example, so let us modify it slightly. We have a $1,000,000 slot machine good for a free play set either to have a chance of .999999 of paying the million or to have a chance of .000001 of paying out the million, you don't know which. There is a $1,000 bill already sitting in the payoff tray. You can either play and keep the thousand or play and return the thousand to the management. The machine was previously set by a psychologist after giving you, for reasons unknown to you, a battery of psychological tests, and so forth as before. The management cannot cheat; there is no way to alter the setting of the machine when you decide whether to return the thousand. So the chances are fixed by the state alone. They are not influenced here by the act as they would be if the management could cheat. Then you should believe that in an infinite sequence of objectively independent repetitions of this experiment (whichever experimental setup it is) the average payoff of the strategy of taking the thousand will exceed the average payoff of the strategy of not taking the thousand by one thousand dollars. In this situation, a frequentist who gets his limit theorems straight will go with the causal decision theorists.

When I said that the idea that the long run argument favors evidential decision theory rests on a *fallacy*, I meant the fallacy of treating uncertainty about chance as if it were certainty about a different chance. If you thought that your *symmetric uncertainty* about the bias of the biased coin was undistinguishable from *knowledge* that the coin was fair, then you might try to apply the law of large numbers for independent and identically distributed trials to conclude that the long-run relative frequency of heads will almost certainly be ½. But this is a *mistake*. A non-trivial mixture of independent sequences is not independent, but only exchangeable. And the appropriate limit theorem is not the strong law of large numbers but rather de Finetti's generalization thereof.

This is not to say that we have a frequentist justification of all of causal decision theory, but we have at least disposed of a bogus justification of evidential decision theory and seen how frequentist questions are properly treated. To go further into the foundations of causal decision theory we must discuss representations.

REPRESENTATIONS

This chapter opened with two concerns about causal considerations in rational decision. The first was that intractable metaphysics might be introduced thereby into the theory of rational decision. The second was that these considerations would wreck the representation theorems for degree of belief that form a foundation for the framework of this book. On examination, the first concern was seen not to constitute a problem. The concept of *chance* already analyzed in chapter 3 provides a framework for a suitable formulation of causal decision theory.

The second does not constitute a problem either. Causal considerations do not constitute any objection to the representation theorem of Bolker, in which states, acts, and consequences are part of one big Boolean algebra and preference is—as Savage suggested—*preference for news items*. To the extent that someone's choice of only the opaque box in the Newcomb problem is evidence for a pre-existing state of the world, it is good news, because it is evidence that the million has been stashed there. The oddity is that the act of taking one box is preferable *qua* news item while the act of taking two boxes is preferable *qua* action, *qua* instrument for effecting consequences. From the standpoint of causal decision theory, the point to be made is just that the systems of Bolker and Jeffrey should not be thought of as logics of decision but rather as logics of a certain kind of preference.

We have preferences for news items. Provided that they fulfill certain coherence conditions and are embeddible in a rich enough structure, we have our representation theorem for degrees of belief and *news values* of propositions. We then have the framework of degrees of belief within which we have been analyzing problems of empiricism. From symmetries in a decision maker's degrees of belief, we can recover *degrees of belief about chance* as in chapter 3. If there are ultimate consequences—propositions which specify everything that the decision maker cares about—then for them, news value and instrumental value coincides. We then have the inputs for causal decision theory. The foundations of causal decision theory are secure.

A more direct representation theorem for causal decision would be desirable for the light that it would throw on the structure of the theory. Recent unpublished work by Armendt[25] gives a representation theorem for Bayesian causal decision theory which identifies the crucial partition, $[K_i]$, of states of the world by the special role of its members in conditional preferences.

CONCLUSION

Newcomb's problem is not so much a paradox as an exercise. It invites us to isolate and compare causal and evidential paradigms for rational decision. For those of us who find the causal paradigm compelling, it invites a general formulation and analysis of causal decision theory. We have seen that the challenges that such a project appear to pose for empiricism turn out not to be real dangers at all. The foundations of the theory of personal probability remain. And the theory can be formulated without the incursion of causal or counterfactual primitives, in terms of the analysis of chance that we have already carried out. Indeed, as we will see in the next chapter, we can turn the problem on its head and use the analysis of chance to give a general Bayesian theory of conditionals.

5 A Bayesian Theory of Subjunctive Conditionals

Even the crows on the rooftops are cawing about the question of which conditionals are true.

attributed to Callimachus
by Sextus Empiricus
Against the Mathematicians[1]

The topic which caused so much discussion in Callimachus' Alexandria is still as controversial as ever. Problems connected with the interpretation of subjunctive conditionals were one of the main stumbling blocks for logical empiricism. We have, however, made *some* progress. While the ancient discussions centered on the material conditional, either unadorned (Philo), or universally quantified over time, or modalized, or some variation on the foregoing ideas,[2] the

---

This chapter grew out of my "Comments on Stalnaker's 'Formal Semantics and Philosophical Problems,'" delivered at the Eastern meetings of the American Philosophical Association in 1979; my discussions of conditionals in my *Causal Necessity* (New Haven and London: Yale University Press, 1980); and my "The Prior Propensity Account of Subjunctive Conditionals," in *Ifs*, ed. Harper et al. (Dordrecht: Reidel, 1981). The results relating Omonotonic families of partitions to Stalnaker selection functions were reported in a paper delivered at the International Congress for Logic Methodology and Philosophy of Science in Salzburg, July 1983.

contemporary discussion has been enriched by two new ideas. I have in mind the Stalnaker-Lewis semantics,[3] in which the truth value of a conditional is determined by the truth value of its consequent in worlds similar to the actual world which make its antecedent true, and the pragmatic conditional probability account, most thoroughly developed by Adams,[4] in which the plausibility of a conditional is identified with the probability of its consequent conditional on its antecedent.

The purpose of this chapter is to formulate a general theory of conditionals, building on the work of Stalnaker, Lewis, and Adams, which has the Stalnaker semantics and the Adams conditional probability account as special cases. The way in which the accounts of Adams and Stalnaker fall out as cases should throw some light on their real relationship.[5] Early on, a simpler strategy for unification of these two approaches was advanced by Ellis[6] and by Stalnaker himself.[7] That is, that conditional probabilities are taken to be the probabilities of truth of conditionals. A famous paper by Lewis showed that this strategy cannot in general succeed.[8] Here we pursue a slightly more complex Bayesian strategy: The basic assertability value of a conditional for an agent is his subjective expectation of the conditional chance of the consequent on the antecedent. Degrees of belief about conditionals are reduced to degrees of belief about conditional chance. These, in turn, are interpreted along the lines of chapter 3.

CHANCE

Allow me to review briefly the fundamental notions in the treatment of unconditional chance before I move to generalize them to conditional chance. In certain typical circumstances in which we are uncertain as to what the chances are, we should take credibility to be the expectation of chance. This is the fundamental Bayesian insight. Remember the example of the biased coin from chapter 3. A coin is to be flipped. It is known to be biased two to one in favor of either heads or tails and that the two alternatives have credibility σ and β respectively. Then our credibility of "The coin will come up heads" should be the credibility weighted average of chance: $\alpha(\frac{2}{3}) + \beta(\frac{1}{3})$.

Suppose that the language on which our credibilities are defined contains the propositions: bias toward heads (BH) and bias toward tails (BT) which are *characteristic* of the chances in that (BH) gets probability one in the chance distribution representing bias toward heads and probability zero otherwise and (BT) gets probability one in the chance distribution representing bias toward tails and zero otherwise. Then, in every one of the credibility distributions gotten by averaging chances as in the last paragraph (with $0 < \alpha < 1$; $\beta = 1 - \alpha$), the two chance distributions can be recovered as probabilities *conditional* on their respective characteristic propositions. In each of these credibility distributions, the credibility of heads conditional on (BH) is equal to $\frac{2}{3}$, which is the chance of heads on the hypothesis of bias toward heads. The propositions [BH, BT] are said to form a *sufficient partition* for the class of credibility distributions under consideration. If credibility is the expectation of chance and the language is rich enough then we can think of chance as credibility conditional on a sufficient partition (or a sufficient sub-sigma algebra).

We can reverse our viewpoint. Starting with credibilities for a language, and a finite partition of that language each of whose members has positive credibility, we can define a random variable—call it "objective chance relative to that partition"—which at every point in our probability space (every "possible world" if you please) takes as its value the probability distribution gotten by conditioning on the member of the partition in which that point lies. The credibility distribution that we started out with is then an average of these "objective chances," and the partition is *sufficient* for the class of probability distributions which are gotten as averages of these "objective chances." If chance is credibility conditional on a partition then the principle that credibility is the expectation of chance follows.

For a certain conception of chances, the dictum that credibility is the expectation of chance only holds in certain epistemic circumstances: roughly, when all our relevant knowledge consists in knowing the possible chances and their credibilities. Suppose that the biased coin of the previous example is to be tossed twice with the tosses objectively independent, and that our credibility for each of the chance distributions is ½. Suppose that someone then tells us that the outcomes of the two tosses do not agree. (We may imagine that this happens after the fact by someone who has seen the trial and is teasing us with a partial report, or before the fact by a clairvoyant or a god or a very good engineer.) After conditionalizing on this report, we have a credibility distribution which cannot be represented as a mixture of the chance distributions in question. And the chances cannot be recovered by conditioning on the partition [BH, BT]. Our new information has complicated the relation of chance to credibility. To recover the chance distributions as probabilities conditional on the partition, we must move back to prior credibilities $[pr_i]$.[9]

The foregoing gives us a *semantics* for chance *relative to a partition*. Let $[b_j]$ be a partition each of whose members have positive credibility in the appropriate credibility distribution $[pr_i]$. The *chance* of a proposition q in world w is taken to be $pr_i(q$ given $b_j)$ where b_j is the member of the partition within which world w lies.

CONDITIONAL CHANCE

The analogous approach to *conditional chance* must be slightly more complicated. If we have a background partition $[b_j]$ such that the intersection of each of its members with proposition p has positive credibility, $pr_i(p \& b_j) \neq 0$, then we can take the conditional chance of q on p in world w to be $pr_i(q$ given $p \& b_j)$ where b_j is the member of the partition which has w as a member. But what if for some j, $pr_i(p \& b_j)$ = 0? Then the appropriate conditional probability is not defined in the standard way. We can see the problem in its irreducible form by considering a regular probability distribution $[pr_i]$ which gives every consistent proposition some positive probability (perhaps infinitesimal). Then our problem arises when the condition, p, is *inconsistent* with some member of the partition. A natural answer, when faced with this problem, is to move to an appropriate partition all of whose members *are* consistent with p. Only the trivial partition, whose only member is the whole space, is consistent with every consistent proposition, p. So a non-trivial semantics for conditional chance must tailor the partition to the condition. *Conditional chance* is given a semantics relative not to one partition but to a *family of partitions*. (More generally, a family of sub-sigma algebras. In this chapter, to avoid obscuring the central ideas with mathematical detail, we will proceed under the simplifying assumptions of regular probability measures and sufficient partitions.)

For example, suppose that the loading of the coin is with iron and that the chances are determined not only by the loading of the coin but also by whether an electromagnet is off or on, thusly:

Chance (Heads)	BH	BT
OFF	$\frac{2}{3}$	$\frac{1}{3}$
ON	$\frac{5}{6}$	$\frac{1}{6}$

Then the conditional chance of heads on a *tautology* is relative to the partition [*BH* & OFF, *BH* & ON, *BT* & OFF, *BT* & ON] and is the same as the unconditional chance of heads relative to that partition. A stronger condition does more of the work and requires less from the background partition. For example, we can plausibly take the chance of heads conditional on ON as relative to the partition [*BH*, *BT*]; and the chance of heads conditional on *BH* as relative to the partition

[ON , OFF]. The former is ⅚ in worlds in BH and ⅙ in worlds in BT; the latter is ⅔ in worlds in OFF and ⅚ in worlds in ON. Supposing that the loading of the coin and whether the electromagnet is on are the only two relevant factors for determining chance at the relevant level of specificity, the appropriate partition for the chance of heads conditional on ON & BH may plausibly be taken as the degenerate partition which has as its only member the whole space (or thinking of it as a proposition, the tautological proposition). Then the conditional chance of heads on the condition ON & BH is ⅚ at every world. The appropriate partition for any condition *stronger* than *ON & BH* (i.e., that entails ON & BH) can also plausibly be taken to be the degenerate partition, since in this case the condition by itself specifies all the appropriate background factors.

This is not to say that the choice of an appropriate partition will always be easy. In real life, various pragmatic factors may be relevant and all of them together may still underdetermine the correct choice. We abstract from these problems by assuming that we have a family of partitions, indexed by the consistent propositions, that does the job. That is, we have a function from consistent propositions to partitions which maps a proposition, p, onto a partition, Π $p = [b_j]$, all of whose members are consistent with p (and such that $pr_i(p \& b_j) \neq 0$ for all j). It would seem natural, given our motivating ideas, to require that such a family have the property that I will call *Omonotonicity*. A family of partitions is *Omonotonic* if whenever p entails q, every member of Π_q whose intersection with p is non-empty is a subset of some member of Π_p. As illustrated in figure 8, in an omonotonic family of partitions, as we move from the weaker condition, q, to the stronger condition, p, we make an appropriate partition, Π_p all of whose members are consistent with p, by first taking all the members of Π_q which are already consistent with p and then "fattening them up" to form a partition by distributing the elements of the other members of Π_q among them.[10]

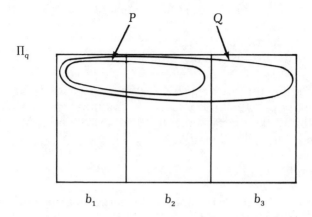

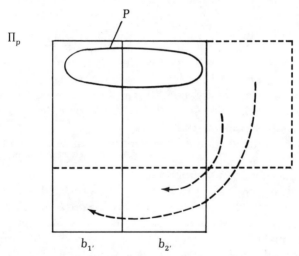

P entail Q. In Π_q we can think of b_1 together with q as determining unconditional chance. *A fortiori*, b_1 together with P determines unconditional chance. Π_q will not serve as an appropriate partition for antecedent P because b_3 is not compatible with P. A natural way to move to a partition appropriate to P is to weaken background conditions b_1 and/or b_2 to $b_{1'}$; $b_{2'}$ so that these now cover all cases originally in b_3.

Figure 8

BASIC ASSERTABILITY VALUE AND
TRUTH VALUES OF CONDITIONALS

Now letting $[pr_i]$ be the prior credibility (in case we need to move to a prior to recover chances) and $[pr_f]$ be the posterior credibility, the theory is that the *Basic Assertability Value* of a conditional, *If p then q*, is:

$$\Sigma_j pr_f(b^p{}_j)\, pr_i(q \text{ given } p \ \& \ b^p{}_j)$$

(where $b^p{}_j$ is the jth member of the partition associated with proposition p). Conditionals in general don't *have* truth values, but in special cases where the antecedent together with the true member of the partition determine the truth value of the consequent we will say that the corresponding conditional has that truth value. That is, if q is true in every world in $p \ \& \ b^p{}_j$ we will say that the conditional, *If p then q*, is true in every world in $b^p{}_j$; likewise for falsity. Then in the special case in which a conditional does have a truth value in every world, Basic Assertability Value coincides with epistemic expectation of truth.

This account does not cover conditionals with inconsistent antecedents. These can remain undefined, or some arbitrary treatment can be imposed.

If we let $[pr_i] = [pr_f]$ and take the degenerate family of partitions which associates with every consistent proposition p, the degenerate partition whose only member is the whole space, then we get the theory proposed for indicative conditionals by Adams and Ellis: i.e., that the basic assertability value for *If p then q* is $pr_f(q \text{ given } p)$. If we keep the degenerate family of partitions but distinguish $[pr_i]$ and $[pr_f]$, we get Adams's treatment of counterfactuals in "Prior Probabilities and Counterfactual Conditionals."[11] If, on the other hand, we have a very rich family of partitions, such that for every consistent p, each member of $[b^p{}_i]$ has exactly one world in $p \ \& \ b_i$, then we make contact with the Stalnaker semantics for subjunctive conditionals. This connection will be explored in the next section. In between the extremes there is a whole range of cases where chance plays its full role.

PARTITIONS AND SELECTION FUNCTIONS

We have, then, a space, Ω, of points (possible worlds), a set, X, of measurable subsets of Ω (propositions) closed under Boolean operations, and two measures on this space, σ and ρ (the first representing our prior probabilities and the second our posterior probabilities). Let P be $X - \Lambda$ (the set of all consistent propositions). Here we avoid complications by assuming regularity of the prior measure: $\rho(p) \neq 0$ for all p ε P. (The space may be finite, or we may have a non-standard measure which allows infinitesimal probabilities.) We assume that the unit set of any point is a proposition: ω ε X for any ω ε Ω. A *family of partitions*, Π, is a function from consistent propositions to partitions, i.e. to sets of members of X whose members are pairwise disjoint and whose union is the whole space, Ω. (Instead of $\Pi(p)$, we write Π_p for the partition that the function Π associates with p) A family of partitions is *Omonotonic* iff whenever p entails q, every member of Π_q consistent with p is a subset of some member of Π_p. A family of partitions is *Deterministic* iff for every p ε P, each member, b, of Π_p is such that b & p contains exactly one point. (Propositions here are sets, so conjunction and set intersection are the same thing.) A *selection function* is a function from $\Omega \times P$ into Ω. It maps pairs of possible worlds and consistent propositions onto possible worlds. A selection function is *Stalnaker* iff (i) $f(\omega, p)$ ε p (ii) If ω ε p then $f(\omega, p) = \omega$. (iii) If $f(\omega, p)$ ε q and $f(\omega, q)$ ε p, then $f(\omega, p) = f(\omega, q)$. The *selection function induced by a Deterministic family of partitions*, Π maps (ω, p) onto that point, ω', which is the sole member of the intersection of p with the element of Π_p which contains ω. (We sometimes write $f(\omega, p)$ as $f_p(\omega)$ when considering p fixed.) Notice that the selection function induced by a Deterministic family of partitions satisfies both conditions (i) and (ii) for being *Stalnaker*.

Theorem I: The selection function induced by a *Determin-istic Omonotonic* family of partitions is *Stalnaker.*

Proof: As noted, (i) and (ii) are satisfied for any selection function induced by a Deterministic family of partitions. We have only to verify that the additional condition of Omono-tonicity leads to condition (iii). Let $f(\omega_1, p) = \omega_2$ and $f(\omega_1, q) = \omega_3$ and $\omega_2 \, \varepsilon \, q$ and $\omega_3 \, \varepsilon \, p$. Then by (i) ω_2 and ω_3 are both in $p \, \& \, q$. By Omonotonicity the member, b, in Π_p which has as members ω_1 and ω_2 and the member, c, in Π_q which has as members ω_1 and ω_3 are subsets of some member, d, of $\Pi_{p\&q}$. By *Determinism*, $\omega_2 = \omega_3$.

The *family of partitions, Π, induced by a Stalnaker selec-tion function, f,* has as elements of Π_p the set of inverse images under f_p of points in p: i.e., $x \, \varepsilon \, p$ iff $f_p^{-1}(x) \, \varepsilon \, \Pi_p$. Note that the family of partitions induced by a Stalnaker selection function is *Deterministic.* Note that the selection function induced by a family of partitions induced by a Stalnaker selection function is the original selection function. Is the family of partitions induced by a Stalnaker selection func-tion always Omonotonic? Or equivalently, is every Stalnaker selection function inducible by an Omonotonic family of partitions?

Theorem II: The family of partitions induced by a Stal-naker selection function is *Deterministic* and *Omonotonic.*

Proof: Determinism is trivial. For Omonotonicity, suppose that p entails q and that there is a b in Π_q and there is a world, ω, in b & p. The set b is then $f_q^{-1}(\omega)$. It is to be shown that b is a subset of some member of Π_p. The required mem-ber is $f_p^{-1}(\omega)$. For if $f_q^{-1}(\omega)$ were not a subset of $f_p^{-1}(\omega)$ there would have to be a point, x in $f_q^{-1}(\omega)$ which is not in $f_p^{-1}(\omega)$. But then $f_q(x)$ which by hypothesis is ω would be in p and $f_p(x)$ would by Stalnaker (i) be in p and thus in q since p entails q. Then by Stalnaker (iii) $f_p(x) = f_q(x) = \omega$, so x is in $f_p^{-1}(\omega)$ after all.

So *every Deterministic Omonotonic family of partitions induces a selection function which is Stalnaker* and *every*

Stalnaker selection function can be induced by a Deterministic Omonotonic family of partitions (by the family that it induces).

CONDITIONALS WITH CHANCE CONSEQUENTS

If we construe chance as credibility conditional on an appropriate partition, then conditionals with chance consequents, If p then Chance (q) = a, are already covered by the preceding theory. The consequent, Chance(q) = a, is a proposition, true in some possible worlds and false in others, and the theory treats it just like any other proposition.

There are, however, several things worth noticing about this special case. We may want the notion of chance used in the consequent to mesh with the notion of conditional chance operative in the definition of basic assertability value for the conditional. This requires coordination of the partition used to define chance with the family of partitions used to define conditional chance. Thus, if we want Chance(q) = a to come out true in just the same worlds as the conditional If tautology, then Chance(q) = a, then we should choose as the partition used for chance either the same partition as or a refinement of that partition which the family assigns to the tautology.

Next, we see that the theory given makes it much easier for conditionals with chance consequents than for conditionals with unqualified consequents to have truth values. Thus, If the magnet is on, then chance of heads is ⅔ may be true in a world although If the magnet is on, then the coin comes up heads lacks a truth value. Indeed, if the partition used to define chance meshes with the family of partitions used to define conditional chance in the appropriate way, then conditionals with chance consequents will always have truth values. The condition which guarantees this is:

MESH: Let Π_p be the partition assigned by the family to p and Π_c be the partition used to objectify chance. For every $p \,\varepsilon\, P$, and every set $b^p{}_i \,\varepsilon\, \Pi_p$, $b^p{}_i$ & p is a subset of c for some $c \,\varepsilon\, \Pi_c$.

Let us illustrate this with our previous example of the coin. Remember:

Ch(H)	BH	BT
OFF	⅔	½
ON	⅚	⅙

The family used to define conditional chance here will map:

Proposition:	onto	Partition
Tautology	[BH & OFF, BH & ON, BT & OFF, BT & ON]	
BH, BT		[ON, OFF]
ON, OFF		[BH, BT]
BH & ON; BH & OFF;		
and any proposition which entails one of these		[Tautology]

The partition used here to define unconditional chance is here [BH & OFF, BH & ON, BT & OFF, BT & ON]; the same as the one that the family of partitions assigns to the tautology. Now at a world in OFF, *If BH then Chance(heads)* = ⅔ is true since the chance of heads as defined is equal to ⅔ at every world which is both in the antecedent, BH, and in the member of the partition associated with the antecedent that the given world is in, i.e., OFF. On the other hand, the conditional with unqualified consequent *If BH then heads* does not have a truth value at that world because *its* consequent is true at some worlds in the set under consideration (BH & OFF) and false in others.

Notice the effect of the way that chance is handled on conditionals of both types with antecedents stronger than the elements of the finest operative partition.

(1) If BH & ON & the coin comes up heads, then the coin comes heads

is true at every world, but:

(2) If BH & ON & the coin comes up heads, then Chance (heads) = 1

is false at every world. Rather

(3) If *BH* & ON & the coin comes up heads, then Chance
(heads) = ⅔

is true at every world. In general, we have: If p & q *then* p as
valid (assuming p & q consistent), but avoid the horrors of:
If p & q then Chance (p) = 1. Resiliency is given its proper
place in the treatment of chance.

ITERATION

The account of conditionals just given requires that the antecedents and consequents of conditionals be *propositions*;
that they can be identified as sets of possible worlds with
well-defined probabilities. Since, according to the account,
conditionals often lack truth values, conditionals cannot in
general be plausibly identified with a set of possible worlds
in which they are true. Too many conditionals with different
assertability values would be identified with the null set of
possible worlds. Consequently, iteration of conditionals is,
in general, problematic. On the other hand, where truth values are well-defined at each possible world, iterations are
already dealt with by the theory. As we have seen in the
preceding section, this happens much more often with subjunctives with chance consequents than with subjunctives
with unqualified consequents.

Where conditionals lack truth values, and iterations lack
even a basic assertability value when taken at face value, we
can sometimes plausibly *impose* a treatment by a slight rein-
terpretation. Where an embedded conditional, *if p then q*,
lacks a truth value, we might substitute for it *The conditional chance of q on p is high* or, putting aside questions of
vagueness, something such as *The conditional chance of q
on p is greater than .95*, which *is* a perfectly respectable
proposition. For example:

If, if Lightning were to run he would win, then the race
would be fixed

becomes:

If the chance of Lightning winning given that he runs were
high, then the race would be fixed.

IMPLICATURE

Throughout, I have been calling what this account gives us *Basic Assertability Value* rather than just assertability value. The reason is that Grice[12] has taught us all that considerations of conversational implicature enter into the determination of overall assertability, and Grice has developed some methodology for separating out considerations of conversational implicature from the rest. What I mean by *Basic Assertability Value* is roughly overall assertability value less conversational implicature. Among conversational implicatures that get separated out in this way, I take the implicature of relevance of the antecedent of a conditional to its consequent. If Sue says to Johnny, "If you come to the party, I'll have a good time," it would be unnatural for him not to assume that his presence would have something to do with her pleasure. But this is only conversational implicature. It can be cancelled—"But if you don't come, I'll have a better time"—without calling the original conditional into doubt. None of the theories of conditionals discussed in this chapter guarantee such relevance and all would do well to avail themselves of the Gricean account.

APPLICATION TO DECISION THEORY

We are now in a position to verify the claims I made in the last chapter about how this Bayesian theory of subjunctive conditionals ties in with the approaches to decision theory of Stalnaker, Gibbard and Harper, and Lewis.

The idea advanced by Stalnaker and developed by Gibbard and Harper is that we get a proper causal decision theory from evidential decision theory by substituting the probability of a conditional for the corresponding conditional probability:

$U(A) = \Sigma_i DB$ (If act A were taken, consequence C would ensue.) Utility (C_i) (where the consequences $[C_i]$ encompass everything of interest to the decision maker).

On the theory of subjunctive conditionals put forward in

this chapter, such conditionals may not have a truth value or a probability of truth, but they always have a basic assertability value. In the deterministic case where they do have a truth value, basic assertability value is equal to degree of belief in the truth of the conditional. Taking $[K_j]$ as the partition which the family assigns to A, assuming that prior to the decision $[pr_i] = [pr_j]$, substituting basic assertability value for degree of belief of the conditional in the Stalnaker-Gibbard-Harper expectation, and generalizing to let the act and state of nature be of concern to the decision maker, we get the Bayesian version of causal decision theory of chapter 4:

$$U(A) = \Sigma_{ij} DB(K_j) \, DB(C_i/A \text{ \& } K) \, U(A \text{ \& } K_j \text{ \& } C_i)$$

The version of causal decision theory advanced by David Lewis[13] is somewhat more complicated, with the conditional probability of evidential decision theory here being replaced with the expectation of the value of chance in a conditional with chance consequent:

$$U(A) = \Sigma_{ij} x_j \, DB(\text{If } A \text{ were the case then Chance } (C_i) \text{ would be } x_j) \, U(C_i)$$

If we make the assumptions we made for Stalnaker-Gibbard-Harper, and assume that for each $i;j$, K_j together with A determines the chance of C_i, we again get back Bayesian causal decision theory. Under these assumptions, the chance of C is constant for worlds in fixed $K \text{ \& } A$, and equal to $DB(C$ given $K \text{ \& } A)$. So:

$$\Sigma_j \, DB(\text{If } A \text{ were the case, then Chance } (C_i) \text{ would be } x_j) = \Sigma_j \, DB \, (C \text{ given } K_j \text{ \& } A)$$

Degrees of belief about subjunctive conditionals with chance consequents yield to degrees of belief conditional on acts and state, and the Lewis theory reduces to Bayesian causal decision theory.[14]

APPLICATION TO QUANTUM THEORY

In quantum theory, the quantum mechanical state together with the measurement made determine the chances of possible measurement results. The physical state of a system corresponds to a normed Hilbert space vector, ψ; the measurement made corresponds to a linear operator, $\hat{A}$, with a complete orthonormal set of eigenvectors $\alpha_1, \alpha_2, \ldots$ The corresponding eigenvalues $A_1, A_2, \ldots$ represent the possible measurement results. The theory tells us how to calculate the chance of a measurement result from the state and the measurement made. (For discrete eigenvalues

Chance $(A_i) = |(\alpha_i, \psi)|^2$

the square of the absolute value of the inner product of the corresponding eigenvector and the state vector.) The quantum mechanical state in this way determines the truth values of conditionals with chance consequents of the form:

If measurement $\hat{A}$ were made, the chance of result A_i would be x.

Suppose that it is just prior to a certain measurement, that you believe quantum theory and have made the requisite calculations, but that you have some uncertainty as to the actual quantum state. The theory of this chapter then applies with the partition of the possible quantum states being the relevant partition for the given antecedent. The conditional from measurement made to chance of measurement result is true or false according to the actual quantum states. Its probability is the sum of the probabilities of the quantum states in which it is true. The conditional with unqualified consequent:

If measurement $\hat{A}$ were made, then result A_i would have ensued

does not have a truth value, since the measurement made together with the quantum state does not determine the measurement result.

Now if I believe quantum theory, I believe that there is some positive but ridiculously small value of x that makes the proposition "If I were to attempt to walk through that wall, the chance that I would succeed would be x" true. The corresponding conditional with unqualified consequent is, strictly speaking, neither true nor false. But, speaking as we do, we will assert the proposition "If I were to attempt to walk through that wall, I would not succeed." Why? It has high *Basic Assertability Value*. The example illustrates the utility of the device of Basic Assertability Value in the economy of thought.

A hidden variable theory for quantum mechanics postulates a finer partition of physical states according to the value of a hidden variable, λ. In a *Deterministic* hidden variable theory, the state together with the measurement made determine the measurement result. A Deterministic hidden variable theory is "counterfactually definite" in that the value of λ determines a truth value for the conditional with unqualified consequent: "If measurement M were made, result R would ensue." In a *stochastic* hidden variable theory, as in quantum theory itself, the physical state together with the measurement made determine only a chance distribution over measurement results. According to stochastic hidden variable theories, λ grounds the truth values of conditionals from measurement made to chance of result, but not corresponding conditionals with unqualified consequent. Stochastic hidden variable theories lack the level of "counterfactual definiteness" of Deterministic theories.

Some commentators on Bell's theorem that every hidden variable theory that reproduces the quantum mechanical statistics must fail to be Bell-local, thought that Bell had smuggled in an illicit premiss of "counterfactual definiteness," and that it therefore did not apply to stochastic hidden variable theories. However, it can be shown that counterfactual definiteness is not smuggled in, but is rather a consequence of the premises adopted for *reductio*. Any stochastic theory that reproduces the quantum statistics and is local in the sense at issue must be deterministic.[15]

CONCLUSION

Subjunctive conditionals can be given a reading free of metaphysical excess. Basic assertability values of subjunctives, like beliefs about unconditional chance, can be explicated in terms of less problematic beliefs. The theory relates subjunctives to conditional chance in a way which explains their function in rational decision and in the statement of physical law.

6 Metaphysics

In the domain of metaphysics . . . *logical analysis yields the negative result that* the alleged statements in this domain are entirely meaningless. *Therewith a radical elimination of metaphysics is attained.* . . .

Rudolf Carnap
"The Elimination of Metaphysics through Logical Analysis of Language"

Let us grant to those who work in a special field of investigation the freedom to use any form of expression which seems useful to them; the work in the field will sooner or later lead to the elimination of those forms which have no useful function. Let us be cautious in making assertions and critical in examining them, but tolerant in permitting linguistic forms.

Rudolf Carnap
"Empiricism, Semantics and Ontology"

The Vienna Circle knew what they wanted to do with metaphysics. They wanted to get rid of it. The problems came in formulating an acceptable form of the verification principle (and an acceptable notion of analyticity) which would suffice for its definition. I have suggested in chapter 1 that many of the difficulties in formulating the verification principle were due to a focus on syntax, and later on syntax and semantics, whereas a proper formulation of the principle is pragmatic. The basic idea of a confirmational theory of significance, when transposed to the theory of personal probability, not only escapes the old difficulties but also has a rationale of its own in terms of the convergence of opinion under the pressure of evidence.

We now have at least a provisional theory of metaphysics: A proposition, *H*, is *empirically meaningful* for *X* at *t* iff there is some evidential proposition, *E*, which is statistically relevant to *H* for *X* at *t*. A proposition has *metaphysical status* for *X* at *t* if it is neither empirically meaningful for *X* at *t* nor *a priori*. Given this sense of metaphysics and some familiarity with the theory of personal probability within which it is formulated, it is now time to reassess the positivists' leading idea. Is metaphysics something that we should strive to eliminate through the yoga of logical analysis?

Is Metaphysics Eliminable?

A proposition's having metaphysical status—being insensitive to all possible evidence—may be due to various reasons, and it is not at the outset clear that all propositions having metaphysical status should be treated in the same way. For instance, you may have a lot of metaphysics in your conceptual system because you are *pigheaded*. You may decide what you think is right and assign it probability one and everything else probability zero. As we saw in chapter 3, one can avoid learning from experience by concentrating one's probability on an extreme point. If your language is full of metaphysical propositions for this reason, you might be well advised to get rid of your metaphysics not by eliminating propositions but by changing their status. Allow some tiny probability that you are wrong and spread it around the other possibilities. Follow Cicero:

> we, however, whose guide is probability and who are unable to advance further than the point at which the likelihood of truth has presented itself, are prepared both to refute without obstinacy and be refuted without anger.[1]

A *sentence* might, in a sense, have metaphysical status for *you* because you simply don't know what it means, and therefore can't figure out what would count as evidence for or against it. You might nevertheless find that you assign a high degree of belief to this sentence, perhaps because it was often repeated in a solemn tone of voice by the elders of your village. Once you realize that you don't know what it means, you should realize that you have no business assigning *it* any degree of belief at all. (This is presumably the sort of case the Vienna Circle had in mind.) You can of course legitimately have a degree of belief in the proposition that the sentence in question expresses some true proposition or other, which might be high or low depending on what you think of the elders of your village, on what attempts you have made to ascertain its meaning, and so forth.

Finally, you may find that your conceptual system contains propositions with metaphysical status because of a disparity in the richness of language of your theories and the language of your evidence. Definitive examples are hard to come by in this area, but the following will at least give an idea of what I have in mind. Suppose that your theoretical language specifies the point at which the center of mass of a body is located, and your observation language permits only finite sequences of measurements of finite accuracy. Suppose that your prior probabilities for the location of the center of mass of a body are absolutely continuous with respect to Lebesgue measure on 3-space, but that this is not a requirement of rationality. Indeed let us suppose that any probability distribution on 3-space is permissible. Then the proposition that the center of mass of the body is at a point with at least one irrational co-ordinate has metaphysical status for you; it has probability one and will have probability one on any possible evidence.

The example is arguable in several ways. Someone might argue that your evidential language should be idealized to include infinite sequences of measurements of arbitrary precision, or that your theoretical language should be replaced by a weaker one. Someone might argue that all rational probability assignments should give this proposition probability one so that it has an *a priori* rather than a metaphysical status. None of these lines has an obvious ring of truth, so let us provisionally accept the example to introduce an issue.

What does seem clear from this example is that we are not likely to get an acceptable theoretical framework simply by starting with the one given and throwing out all propositions with metaphysical status. Even an ultra-empiricist who wants a weaker theoretical language will presumably not attempt to find his candidate in this way. He will look at the question of the language as a whole, and select his framework paying attention to broadly pragmatic considerations.

But, as we all know, from this standpoint ultra-empiricism doesn't do too well. Mathematically rich languages appear to be required for fruitful scientific theories. It appears here that we have *metaphysics that shouldn't be eliminated* either by eliminating the propositions in question or by eliminating their metaphysical status.

If so and if, as I suggested in chapter 1, propositions with metaphysical status for you are not propositions that you can *know*, then you *ought* to have propositions in your conceptual system which are not candidates for knowledge. This is a surprising epistemological thesis, but it follows from plausible principles.

At the very least, we can say that the eliminability of metaphysics of the type in question can't be taken for granted. Now that we have a definition of metaphysics, questions of the eliminability of metaphysics in any area with a rich theoretical structure will raise substantive mathematical questions: What sort of structure would be left if the propositions with metaphysical status were excluded piecemeal? What sort of languages are available for wholesale substitution, such that none of their propositions will have metaphysical status? In short, the eliminability of metaphysics in a given area would have to be a *theorem*, rather than a piece of philosophical doctrine.

ARE EMPIRICALLY MEANINGFUL PROPOSITIONS ELIMINABLE?

Consider, however, statements of *chance*. If you are not pig-headed, statements of chance *will* be empirically meaningful for you. Evidence will be relevant to your degrees of belief concerning the chances as discussed in chapter 3. But we also saw in chapter 3 that statements about chance are, in a sense, eliminable *via* generalizations of de Finetti's representation theorem. Under the conditions of these representation theorems, one who has degrees of belief on a language from which all mention of chance has been removed behaves *as if* he had degrees of belief in chance propositions and his degrees of belief in assertoric propositions were the epistemic expectation of chance. The whole structure of degrees of belief about chances emerges as an artifact of the representation. Thus there is a precisely delimited sense in which the elimination of statements of chance incurs *no theoretical cost*.[2] This is not in general true for theoretical statements, *or even for statements with metaphysical status*. Statements of chance are as eliminable as we have a right to expect anything to be. So some cognitively meaningful statements are eliminable.

We can perhaps find other examples as well. In chapter 5, I sketched a treatment of subjunctive conditionals analogous to the treatment of chance in chapter 3. I suggested briefly in chapter 3 and argued at length in a previous book[3] that the necessity of laws is captured by *resiliency* and thus that the concept of causal necessity is eliminable as well. Significant eliminability results may be found in other areas.[4]

The notion of eliminability is pragmatic and holistic. To say that a proposition or set of propositions is eliminable from a language is to say that if they are eliminated the language can fulfill certain functions just as well. Eliminability will depend on what functions we take to be salient. In discussing the eliminability of chance we gave an account of the function of chance in statistical inference, and then argued that that function can be fulfilled even if our language does not contain explicit reference to chance. Eliminability is holistic in that it depends on the relation of the propositions under consideration for elimination to the language as a whole, not just to that part of the language which encodes the evidence. The notion of metaphysical status is more circumscribed. It depends only on the evidential part of the language, and only on the degree-of-belief relationships between that sublanguage and the proposition or propositions in question. Both are interesting and important concepts (or families of concepts), but they are distinct. In the early days of logical empiricism there was some tendency to conflate the two. Later, in "Empiricism, Semantics, and Ontology," Carnap was concerned with many of the considerations we have found salient to eliminability.

EVIDENCE

Empirical meaningfulness depends on what propositions we take as representing possible evidence. There is, however, the worry that by assuming that evidence can be represented by propositions at all we may be compromising the fallibilist and probabilist spirit of this enquiry. I have said something about these concerns in chapter 2, but I think that it is time to say something more.

In chapter 2, I suggested that the introduction of higher-order degrees of belief eases the problem of uncertain evidence. Instead of my epistemic input being either "That is an avocet" or "That isn't an avocet," it can be "The observational probability that that is an avocet is nine out of ten," etc.[5] Likewise for "This patch of color appears blue." We are not forced to assume that there is an observation language describing the world, such that observations confer certainty on observational propositions. Rather we can have a model in which observations affect the probabilities of observational propositions in a way that stops short of pushing those probabilities to zero or one, in which our *evidential* language is not the observation language itself but rather one which describes probabilities on the observation language.

We can push the treatment of uncertain observations a bit further. To fix a point of view, suppose that you as engineering epistemologist are analyzing a probabilistic automaton. The automaton has a high-level language which you find fruitful for analyzing the way in which it processes information. It also has a low-level "machine language." The automaton has a peripheral "observation device" for detecting various heart abnormalities. The peripheral consists of an electrocardiograph and a microprocessor. After an observation it feeds the central processing unit of the automaton "observational probabilities" of various types of heart abnormality. The central processing unit contains a medical history of the patient together with records of previous electrocardiograms, and from these together with the input from its peripheral computes final probabilities.

If you are talking about the epistemic input for the central processing unit from the peripheral, you talk about the observational probabilities. In so describing them you are talking a high-level language. They also have a realization in the machine language. You could also look at the input for the microprocessor in the peripheral, or the input for the whole system at the electrodes of the electrocardiograph. These inputs may have no description in the high-level language of the central processor but have a description in a low-level "nuts and bolts" language of the whole system. What is the "real" language of the system? Both are.

In observation, for us or the automaton, there is always something that happens, something that is the epistemic input. It might have a precise description not at the level of the language of our conscious thought but only at the level of the language of the optic nerve. So if we push these skeptical considerations far enough, it may turn out that from the standpoint of the language of conscious thought the observation language consists of hidden variables.

Then at this level of epistemological nicety, the relevance of an agent's epistemic inputs to her, his, or its degrees of belief in a proposition may be a question that the agent in question is in no position to answer. Questions as to which propositions have epistemological status for this agent are ultimately questions properly referred to the agent's psycho-physicoepistemological engineer.

Having said this, I should also say that at a less rarified level of analysis we can do quite a bit as our own epistemological engineers, and that the consideration of observational probabilities as inputs helps us to do more.

PRAGMATICS AND EMPIRICISM

The Vienna Circle thought that statements which had metaphysical status according to the verifiability criterion must be eliminable and should be eliminated. They thought that sentences with metaphysical status were really just gobbledegook, that they had no cognative meaning at all. This conception of metaphysics was due perhaps to an unduly narrow view of the ways in which a statement can have metaphysical status.

Given our version of the verifiability criterion, we have *prima facie* examples of metaphysics that are not eliminable, and of cognitively meaningful statements that are. The notions of metaphysical status and of eliminability are both of epistemological importance. Statements with metaphysical status, being supported neither by evidence nor by reason, have no claim to being *knowledge*. It appears that some statements with metaphysical status are not eliminable, and for them the most severe moral that we can draw is that they should be recognized for what they are.

On the other hand we have a variety of statements which are empirically meaningful[6] and which are eliminable: statements of chance, subjunctive conditionals, and the like. To say that they are eliminable is not to say that we ought to eliminate them. Humeans who know the ergodic representation can speak of chance in good conscience, knowing in their hearts that they are committed to nothing more than subjective probability. Proof of eliminability is, for them, a reason *not* to eliminate. We should, I suppose, eliminate gobbledegook from our language and pigheadedness from our way of thinking, but I can see no good reason for eliminating all eliminable propositions.

This pragmaticized version of empiricism is, in the spirit of Carnap's later work, accommodating but discriminating. It is not the kind of positivism with only two categories: "observable" and "other." Evidential statements may include not only descriptions of observables but also specifications of observational probabilities. Empirically significant statements may include as well many theoretical statements of science: statements about electrons or fields or quantum states. Fruitful theories may require an uneliminable residue of metaphysics. Where we have eliminability, it is something to be proved rather than something to be taken as an item of doctrine. There is room in this version of empiricism for all of science, and the means to recognize the various kinds of propositions which occur in science for what they truly are.

Notes

CHAPTER 1

1. "Soziologie im Physicalismus," *Erkentniss* 2 (1931)/32), trans. as "Sociology and Physicalism" in *Logical Positivism*, ed. A. J. Ayer (New York: Free Press, 1959), 282–317. The references to "experience as a whole" and "the given" are directed at Schlick.
2. R. Carnap, *Logische Syntax der Sprach* (Vienna: Springer Verlag, 1934) trans. as *The Logical Syntax of Language* (New York: Harcourt Brace, 1937).
3. R. Carnap, "Intellectual Autobiography," in *The Philosophy of Rudolf Carnap*, ed. P. A. Schlipp, The Library of Living Philosophers (Open Court, Glencoe, Ill. 1963).
4. And in a certain setting sufficient. See C. Smorynski, "The Incompleteness Theorems," in *Handbook of Mathematical Logic*, ed. J. Barwise (Amsterdam: North Holland, 1970), 819–65.
5. Reprinted as an appendix to C. Reid, *Hilbert* (Berlin: Springer Verlag, 1970).
6. "The Empiricist Criterion of Meaning," *Revue Internationale de Philosophie* 4 (1950), reprinted in *Logical Positivism*, ed. A. J. Ayer (New York: Free Press, 1959), 116.
7. Translated as "The Concept of Truth in Formalized Languages," in A. Tarski, *Logic, Semantics, and Metamathematics* (Oxford: Oxford University Press, 1956).
8. A. Tarski, A. Mostowski, and R. Robinson, *Undecidable Theories* (Amsterdam: North Holland, 1953).
9. See B. Russell, and A. N. Whitehead, *Principia Mathematica*, 2nd ed., especially the preface to the second edition and appendix C. The principle of supervenience is expressed here by saying that every proposition is a *truth function* (perhaps infinitary) of the basic ones.
10. Assuming here that identity is, for observable objects, an observable relation.

11. The foregoing is not intended to be a comprehensive account of van Fraassen's views. His position on the vagueness and theory-laden character of "observable" is complex, and I will not attempt to discuss it here. See van Fraassen, *The Scientific Image* (Oxford: Clarendon Press, 1980).

12. C. G. Hempel, "The Empiricist Criterion of Meaning," sec 3.

13. R. Carnap, "Testability and Meaning," *Philosophy of Science* 3 (1936): 420–68.

14. R. Carnap, "The Methodological Character of Theoretical Concepts," in *Minnesota Studies in the Philosophy of Science*, vol. 1, ed. H. Feigl and M. Scriven (Minneapolis: University of Minnesota Press, 1956).

15. F. P. Ramsey, "Theories," in *The Foundations of Mathematics* (New York: Harcourt Brace, 1931).

16. R. Carnap, *The Philosophy of Rudolf Carnap*, ed. P. A. Schilpp, The Library of Living Philosophers (Glencoe, Ill.: Open Court: 1963); and R. Carnap, *Philosophical Foundations of Physics*, ed. M. Gardner (New York: Basic Books, 1966).

17. See J. Sneed, *The Logical Structure of Mathematical Physics* (Dordrecht: Reidel, 1971).

18. R. Carnap, *Philosophical Foundations of Physics*, 226.

19. R. Carnap, *The Philosophy of Rudolf Carnap*, 861.

20. For sophisticated modal relative frequency interpretations, see H. Kyburg, "Propensities and Probabilities," *British Journal for Philosophy of Science* 25 (1974): 358–75; and B. van Fraassen, "Relative Frequencies," *Synthese* 34 (1977): 133–66.

21. R. Carnap, "Reply to Henle," in *The Philosophy of Rudolf Carnap*. Reichenbach's formulation is somewhat different: ". . . a proposition has meaning if it is possible to determine a weight, i.e. a degree of probability, for the proposition." H. Reichenbach, *Experience and Prediction* (Chicago: University of Chicago Press, 1938), 54.

22. Violating Hempel's criterion of adequacy (A) of "Empiricist Criteria of Cognitive Significance: Problems and Changes," in *Aspects of Scientific Explanation* (New York: Free Press, 1965), 331–496.

CHAPTER 2

1. See S. Sambursky, "On the Possible and the Probable in Ancient Greece," *Osiris* 12 (1956): 35–48; D. Garber and S. Zabell, "On

the Emergence of Probability," *Archive for History of the Exact Sciences* 21, no. 1 (1979): 33–53; F. N. David, *Games, Gods, and Gambling* (New York: Hafner, 1962).

2. F. P. Ramsey, "Truth and Probability," in *The Foundations of Mathematics and Other Essays* (Paterson, N.J.: Littlefield Adams & Co., 1960), 157–198.

3. We assume here the constant marginal utility of money; or that the payoffs are in units of utility. For a deeper justification which does not require such assumptions we must move to the probability-utility representation theorems to be discussed in the next section.

4. More precisely, by a *betting arrangement*, I mean a function, B, from possible states of affairs to payoffs. A *bet* on a proposition, p, is a betting arrangement which has a gain, a, associated with every state of affairs in p and a loss, b, associated with every state of affairs not in p. The *aggregate* of two betting arrangements, $B_1 \# B_2$, is the betting arrangement which has at each possible state of affairs, w, the sum of the payoffs at w of the constituent bets, B_1; B_2:

$$B_1 \# B_2(w) = B_1(w) + B_2(w)$$

Probability is to perform the practical function of placing a value, *expected value*, on bets and betting arrangements when the agent is uncertain as to the state of the world. Expected value *is* the value of a betting arrangement; we assume that an agent will be agreeable to selling a betting arrangement with expected value X for one with expected value X or more, or to buying it for one with expected value X or less.

Then expected value should be additive over aggregation. Assume (1) The bet "V for sure," which returns the value V in every possible circumstance, has value V; and (2) If $EV(B_1') = EV(B_1)$ and $EV(B_2') = EV(B_2)$ then $EV(B_1 \# B_2) = EV(B_1' \# B_2')$. Then for any two betting arrangements, B_1; B_2, let B_1' be the bet which returns $V = EV(B_1)$ for sure; likewise for B_2' and B_2. Then $EV(B_1 \# B_2) = EV(B_1' \# B_2')$ by (2). (You can sell B_1 for B_1' and B_2 for B_2' and have an arrangement of equal value.) And $EV(B_1' \# B_2') = EV(B_1') + EV(B_2')$ by (1) and the definition of the aggregate of two bets. And $EV(B_1') = EV(B_1)$ and $EV(B_2') = EV(B_2)$ by (1). So we have additivity over aggregation: $EV(B_1 \# B_2) = EV(B_1) + EV(B_2)$.

Now if propositions p and q are incompatible, it is a matter of elementary truth-functional logic that the aggregate of a bet B_1 ($1 if p, nothing otherwise) and a bet B_2 ($1 if q, nothing otherwise) is a bet on the proposition p or q ($1 if p or q, nothing otherwise). But the expected values of these bets are just the probabilities of the corresponding propositions:

$$Pr(p \text{ or } q) = Pr(p) + Pr(q)$$

5. F. P. Ramsey, "Truth and Probability," 182.
6. For instance, R. Jeffrey's Ph.D. dissertation, "Contributions to the Theory of Inductive Probability" (Princeton University, 1957); S. Spielman, "Physical Probability and Bayesian Statistics," *Synthese* 36 (1977): 235–69; B. Skyrms, "Zeno's Paradox of Measure," in *Physics, Philosophy, and Psychoanalysis*, ed. R. S. Cohen and L. Lauden (Dordrecht: Reidel, 1983), 223–54; T. Seidenfeld and M. J. Schervish, "A Conflict between Finite Additivity and Avoiding Dutch Book," *Philosophy of Science* 50 (Sept. 1983): 398–412.

   In terms of my version of the coherence argument for finite additivity of the preceding footnote, we define the *aggregate*, $\#_i B_i$, of a countable number of bets; $B_1, B_2, \ldots$, as the betting arrangement which has at each possible state of affairs, w, the sum of the payoffs associated with each of the constituent bets:

   $$\#_i B_i(w) = \Sigma_i B^i(w)$$

   We can then argue, just as before, that expected value should be countably additive over countable aggregation; that the countable aggregate of bets ($1 if p_i, nothing otherwise) or pairwise incompatible propositions is the corresponding bet on the countably infinite disjunction, and thus that the only way to consistently evaluate such bets is by countably additive probabilities.
7. To be precise, in the half-open interval $[0, \frac{1}{2})$ of the race course of unit length.
8. It should be noted, however, that the foregoing argument for countable additivity proceeded under the presumption of real-valued probabilities, values and expected values. If one allows infinitesimals *via* the techniques of non-standard analysis then the infinite sum—the limit of the sequence of finite partial sums—may not even exist. So this is *not* an argument against non-standard representations of degrees of belief. It is an argument that standard representations should be countably additive. See

A. Bernstein and F. Wattenburg, "Nonstandard Measure Theory," in W. A. J. Luxemburg, ed. *Applications of Model Theory to Algebra, Analysis, and Probability* (New York: Holt, Rinehart, & Winston, 1969), 171–85.

9. B. de Finetti, "La Prevision: ses lois logiques, ses sources subjectives," *Annales de l'institute Henri Poincaré* 7 (1937), trans. in Kyburg and Smokler, eds., *Studies in Subjective Probability* (New York: 1964), 109. For an elementary treatment, see my *Choice and Chance*, 2nd ed. (Belmont, California: Wadsworth, 1975) chap. 6.

10. F. P. Ramsey, "Truth and Probability," 192.

11. See D. Freedman and R. Purves, "Bayes' Method for Bookies," *Annals of Mathematical Statistics* 40 (1969): 177–86, and the argument of David Lewis, reported in P. Teller, "Conditionalization and Observation," *Synthese* (1973): 218–58.

12. L. J. Savage, *The Foundations of Statistics* (New York: 1954) (2nd rev. ed. New York: Dover, 1972); E. D. Bolker, "A Simultaneous Axiomatization of Utility and Subjective Probability," *Philosophy of Science* 34 (1967): 333–40; R. D. Luce and D. H. Krantz, "Conditional Expected Utility," *Econometrica* 39 (1971): 253–71. We should also mention Z. Domotor, "Axiomatization of Jeffrey Utilities," *Synthese* 39 (1978): 165–210, which allows nonstandard probability representations. There are useful surveys of various approaches in T. Fine, *Theories of Probability* (New York: Academic Press, 1973), chap. 2; in D. Krantz, R. D. Luce, P. Suppes, A. Tversky, *Foundations of Measurement*, vol. 1 (New York: Academic Press, 1971) chap. 5; and in P. Fishburn, "Subjective Expected Utility: A Review of Normative Theories" *Theory and Decision* 13 (1981): 139–199. Regarding countable additivity in qualitative probability representations, see C. Villegas, "On Qualitative Probability σ-algebras," *Annals of Mathematical Statistics* 35 (1964): 1787–96.

13. L. J. Savage, *Foundations of Statistics*, 33.

14. B. Ellis, *Rational Belief Systems*, APQ Library of Philosophy (Oxford: Basil Blackwell, 1979).

15. E.g. D. Miller, "A Paradox of Information," *British Journal for Philosophy of Science* 17 (1966), which turns on a de dicto–de re ambiguity. See the discussion in my "Higher Order Degrees of Belief," in *Prospects for Pragmatism*, ed. D. H. Mellor (Cambridge University Press: Cambridge, 1980), from which this section is largely drawn.

16. B. de Finetti, *Probability, Induction, and Statistics* (London: Wiley, 1972), 189.
17. F. P. Ramsey, "Truth and Probability," 169–171.
18. B. de Finetti, *Probability, Induction, and Statistics*, 189.
19. For a discussion related to this case, see R. Jeffrey, "Preference among Preferences," *Journal of Philosophy* 63 (1974): 377–91.
20. L. J. Savage, *The Foundations of Statistics*, 31.
21. "One tempting representation of the unsure is to replace a person's single probability measure P by a set of such measures, especially a convex set. . . ." *The Foundations of Statistics*, 2nd ed., 58.
22. D. Bernoulli, "Specimen Theorae Novae de Mensura Sortis," *Commentarii Academiae Scientiarum Imperialis Petropolitanea* 5 (1738): 175–92, trans. as "Exposition of a New Theory on the Measurement of Risk" by Louise Sommer in *Enconometrica* 22 (1954): 23–26.
23. See M. Allais, "Le comportment de l'homme rationnel devant le risque: critique des postulats et axiomes de l'école américaine," *Econometrica* 21 (1953): 503–46; D. Ellsberg, "Risk, Ambiguity, and the Savage Axioms," *The Quarterly Journal of Economics* 75 (1961): 670–89; W. Fellner, "Distortion of Subjective Probabilities as a Reaction to Uncertainty," *The Quarterly Journal of Economics* (75): 670–89; and Savage's discussion in *The Foundations of Statistics*.
24. R. Jeffrey, *The Logic of Decision*.
25. See my "Higher Order Degrees of Belief" (1980). I. J. Good makes the same point independently in "The Weight of Evidence Provided by an Uncertain Testimony or from an Uncertain Event," *Journal of Statistical Computation and Simulation* 13 (1981): 56–60.
26. See my "Higher Order Degrees of Belief" (1980) and my "Maximum Entropy Inference as a Special Case of Conditionalization," *Synthese* (forthcoming).
27. I. J. Good, *The Estimation of Probabilities: An Essay on Modern Bayesian Methods* (Cambridge, Mass.: MIT Press, 1965) and elsewhere.
28. *Trabajos de Estradistica e Investigacion Operativa*, vol. 31 (*Bayesian Statistics*) ed. J. M. Bernardo, M. H. DeGroot, D. V. Lindley, A. F. M. Smith, (Valencia, Spain: University Press, 1980), 505.

29. See the articles by I. J. Good and J. M. Dickey in *Bayesian Statistics* (n. 28 above) and the ensuing discussion and the references cited there.

CHAPTER 3

1. εικοτολογια. This is a degree-of-belief notion of probability. See Socrates' discussion of εικοσ in *Phaedrus* 273, and S. Sambursky, "On the Possible and the Probable in Ancient Greece." *Osiris* 12 (1956): 35–48.

2. Thus Mill in *A System of Logic*: "The universe, so far as is known to us, is so constituted, that whatever is true in any one case, is true in all cases of a certain description; the only difficulty is to find out what description."

3. As the "grue-bleen" paradox.

4. Probability one for an infinite sequence.

5. The result for infinite sequences and a powerful notion of randomness is in P. Martin-Löf, "The Definition of a Random Sequence," *Information and Control* 9 (1966): 602–19. The analogous theorem for the finite approximation is in T. Fine, "On the Apparent Convergence of Relative Frequency and Its Implications," *Institute of Electrical and Electronic Engineers Transactions Information Theory* IT-16 (1970): 251–57. See also the discussion of this point in T. Fine, *Theories of Probability* (New York: Academic Press, 1973), p. 93 and chap. 5. There are two main approaches to defining a random sequence, the approach requiring the sequence to pass all recursive statistical tests of randomness and the approach based on computational complexity. The first trivially requires convergence to a limiting relative frequency. Less trivially, it can be shown that for a suitably chosen computational-complexity definition of randomness, any sequence that is random in that sense is random in the statistical-test sense. Fine's theorem shows that for finite sequences, approximate randomness in the computational-complexity sense at suitable level guarantees the desired level of approximate convergence.

6. One which is thoroughly discussed in A. Burks, *Cause, Chance, and Reason* (Chicago: University of Chicago Press, 1979).

7. So pr_{BH}(heads on toss 1) = $\frac{2}{3}$, pr_{BT} (heads on toss 1) = $\frac{1}{3}$; pr_{BH} (heads on toss 1 and heads on toss 2) = $(\frac{2}{3})^2$, etc.

8. Exchangeability.

9. The epistemic probability of two heads = $5/18$ = the epistemic probability of two tails. That of one head and one tail (in any order) = $4/9$.

10. I.e. if our *epistemic* distribution took this form, our reasoning would, in a sense, be counterinductive.

11. "Mixture" now includes continuously weighted averages: $\int p \, du$.

12. I.e., the mixing measure, the weight of the weighted average, is unique. In our example of coin flipping, in each trial there are two possible outcomes, so we can think of this case as that of a sequence of random variables taking the values zero and one. De Finetti proved the representation theorem for this case, and generalized it to the case of a sequence of real-valued random variables. However, if the random variables take their values in a sufficiently mathematically ill-behaved space, the theorem can fail, as is shown in L. Dubins and D. A. Freedman, "Exchangeable Processes Need Not Be Mixtures of Independent Identically Distributed Random Variables," *Zeitschrift fur Wahrscheinlichkeitstheorie und verwandte Gebiete* 48(1979): 115–32. It suffices for the theorem that the random variables take their values in a standard Borel space (a probability space that is Borel-isomorphic to a Borel subset of a complete separable metric space). See E. B. Dynkin, "Sufficient Statistics and Extreme Points," *Annals of Probability* 6 (1978): 705–30. Throughout this chapter we will make the modest regularity assumption that we are dealing with standard Borel spaces.

13. This is basically a consequence of the law of large numbers for independent trials together with Bayes' theorem.

14. Or any of the finite extremal hypergeometric distributions except the one corresponding to all heads and no tails.

15. P. Diaconis, "Finite Forms of de Finetti's Theorem on Exchangeability," *Synthese* 36 (1977): 271–81; P. Diaconis, and D. Freedman, "Finite Exchangeable Sequences," *Annals of Probability* vol. 8, no. 4 (1980): 745–64; P. Diaconis, and D. Freedman, "De Finetti's Generalizations of Exchangeability," in *Studies in Inductive Logic and Probability II*, ed. R. C. Jeffrey (Berkeley and Los Angeles: University of California Press, 1980), 233–49.

16. Let PR be an exchangeable probability measure on sequences of zeros and ones of length r, that is extendable to an exchangeable

probability measure on sequences of length k, $(k > r)$. Then there is a mixing measure, μ, such that for any set A in $(0, 1, \ldots r)$, the error in the representation, i.e. the absolute value of

PR(number of ones in k trials is in A)—

$$\sum_{j \varepsilon A} \binom{r}{j} \int_0^1 p^j(1-p)^{r-j}\, d\,\mu\,(p)$$

is no greater than $2r/k$.

17. The "gambler's fallacy" in its usual form is a bit different. The gambler reasons that he has a fixed finite number of gambles in his lifetime and a fixed finite number of wins. He correctly sees that in the hypergeometric distribution corresponding to these numbers, a loss raises the probability of subsequent wins. Since he is uncertain about these numbers, his epistemic probability will be a mixture, and he incorrectly assumes that negative statistical relevance in each of the elements of the mixture implies negative statistical relevance in the mixture.

18. More generally, to predict the result of the next toss after observing N tosses of which the h have been heads, the counter-inductivist might adopt the hypergeometric distribution corresponding to an urn in which there are $N + 1$ balls of which h are heads if $h > N - h$; of which $h + 1$ are heads otherwise.

19. Some philosophers would think this not odd, but normal.

20. B. de Finetti, "Sur la condition d'équivalence partielle," *Actualités Scientifiques et Industrielles* 739 (Paris: Hermann & Cie, 1938), trans. as "On the Condition of Partial Exchangeability," in *Studies in Inductive Logic and Probability II*, ed. R. Jeffrey (Berkeley and Los Angeles: University of California Press, 1980) 197.

21. B. de Finetti, "On the Condition of Partial Exchangeability," 198.

22. B. de Finetti, *Theory of Probability*, vol. 2 (New York: 1975), 212.

23. P. Diaconis and D. Freedman, "De Finetti's Generalizations of Exchangeability," in Jeffrey, ed., *Studies in Inductive Logic and Probability II*, 233–49.

24. Here we have finite one-sided sequences in mind.

25. D. Freedman, "Invariants under Mixing Which Generalize de Finetti's Theorem," *Annals of Mathematical Statistics* 33 (1962): 916–23.

26. P. Diaconis and D. Freedman, "De Finetti's Generalizations of Exchangeability."

27. It is a convex set in the appropriate vector space of measures.

28. By a degenerate mixture, I mean a weighted average that puts all its weight on one element.

29. P. Diaconis and D. Freedman, "De Finetti's Generalizations of Exchangeability."

30. P. Diaconis and D. Freedman, "De Finetti's Theorem for Markov Chains," *Annals of Probability* 8 (1980): 115–30.

31. I.e. when the probability that the initial state occurs infinitely often is one.

32. B. de Finetti, "On the Condition of Partial Exchangeability."

33. G. Link, "Representation Theorems of the de Finetti Type for (Partially) Symmetric Probability Measures," in Jeffrey, ed., *Studies in Inductive Logic and Probability II,* 207–31.

34. P. Diaconis and D. Freedman, "De Finetti's Generalizations of Exchangeability."

35. C. Preston, *Random Fields* Lecture Notes in Mathematics 534 (Berlin: Springer Verlag, 1976).

36. H. O. Georgii, *Canonical Gibbs Measures* Lecture Notes in Mathematics 760 (Berlin: Springer Verlag, 1976).

37. A standard Borel space is a Borel space that is Borel-isomorphic to the Borel space defined by a Borel subset of a complete separable metric space.

38. As we learn from experience by converging on one of the possible chance distributions, we learn (with probability one in the limit) which of the invariant sets we are in. This justifies the use of the word "projectible."

39. Billingsley suggests that we think of the measure-preserving transformations as representing the repetition of an experiment which leaves the chance structure unchanged in P. Billingsley, *Ergodic Theory and Information* (New York: Wiley, 1965). There are some tantalizing remarks about the relation of propensity to ergodicity by A. Shimony in his introduction to R. Carnap, *Two Essays on Entropy* (Berkeley and Los Angeles: University of California Press, 1977), xvii, together with reference to a projected article, "The Propensity Interpretation of Probability," by K. Friedman and A. Shimony. This paper is not available as I write. After this manuscript was completed, I became aware of two papers by J. von Plato suggesting that ergodic probabilities should be used for the explication of physical probability. See

J. von Plato, "The Significance of the Ergodic Decomposition of Stationary Measures for the Interpretation of Probability," *Synthese* 53 (1982): 419–32, and "The Method of Arbitrary Functions" *British Journal for the Philosophy of Science* 34 (1983): 37–47. These writers do not, however, advocate the subjectivistic line that I put forward here.

40. G. D. Birkhoff, "Proof of the Ergodic Theorem," *Proceedings of the National Academy U.S.A.* 17 (1931): 656–60.

41. N. Kryloff and N. Bogoliouboff, "La théorie générale de la mesure dans son application a l'étude des systemes dynamiques de la mécanique non-linéaire," *Annals of Mathematics* 2nd ser. 38 (1937): 65–113. See also the account in J. C. Oxtoby, "Ergodic Sets," *Bulletin of the American Mathematical Society* 58 (1952): 116–30.

42. More generally, under these conditions, if f is an integrable function, then its limiting empirical average:

$$\lim_{n \to \infty} 1/n \sum_{k=0}^{n-1} f\left(T^k \omega\right)$$

exists almost everywhere. Considered as a point function on Ω, the limiting empirical average is integrable, invariant, and has expectation equal to the expectation of f.

If the transformation is, in addition, ergodic with respect to P, then the limiting relative frequency is almost everywhere constant and equal to the probability and the limiting empirical average is almost everywhere constant and equal to the expectation of f.

43. Birkhoff put forward in the "Hypothesis of Metrical Transitivity" that it is true in general for Hamiltonian systems that Liouville measure restricted to a constant energy hypersurface is ergodic. This hypothesis is shown to be false by the work of Kolmogoroff, Arnold and Moser. See J. Moser, *Stable and Random Motions in Dynamical Systems* (Princeton: Princeton University Press, 1973); and L. Markus and K. Meyer, *Generic Hamiltonian Dynamical Systems are neither Integrable nor Ergodic* (Providence: American Mathematical Society, 1974). However, on the positive side, Sinai has shown this sort of ergodicity for a system of elastic spheres. See Y. Sinai, "Dynamical Systems with Elastic Reflections," *Russian Mathematical Surveys* 25 (1970): 137–89.

44. Let $f(\omega)$ be one if the random variable, f, takes a value in s, a measurable subset of S, and zero otherwise. Then

$$1/n \sum_{k=1}^{n-1} f\left(T^k\omega\right)$$

is the relative frequency of s in the sequence of trials $f_1, f_2, \ldots,$ f_n. According to the ergodic theorem the limiting relative frequency almost everywhere exists and is equal to the probability that the outcome of trial one is in s.

45. For a characterization of the ergodic Markov shifts, see P. Billingsley, *Ergodic Theory and Information*, 31–33.

46. D. Freedman, "Invariants Generalizing de Finetti's Theorem."

47. On the role of the invariant sets as a sufficient sub-sigma algebra, see R. H. Farrell, "Representation of Invariant Measures," *Illinois Journal of Mathematics* 6 (1962): 447–67; and E. B. Dynkin, "Sufficient Statistics and Extreme Points," *Annals of Probability* 5 (1978): 705–30.

CHAPTER 4

1. As for Deliberation, do people deliberate about everything—are all things possible objects of deliberation—, or are there some things about which deliberation is impossible? The term "object of deliberation" presumably must not be taken to include things about which a fool or a madman might deliberate, but to mean what a sensible person might deliberate about.

    Well then, nobody deliberates about things eternal, such as the order of the universe, or the incommensurability of the diagonal and the side of a square. Nor yet about things that change but follow a regular process, whether from necessity or by nature or through some other cause: such phenomonae for instance as the solstices and the sunrise. Nor about irregular occurrences, such as droughts and rains. Nor about the results of chance, such as finding a hidden treasure. The reason that we do not deliberate about these things is that none of them can be effected by our agency.

    Aristotle, *Nichomachean Ethics* III, iii, 1–6, trans. H. Rackham (The Loeb Classical Library) (London: Heinemann, 1926).

2. J. Tinbergen, *On the Theory of Economic Policy* (Amsterdam: N. Holland, 1955). The *data variables, target variables,* and *instrument variables* of chapter 2 correspond roughly to states, consequences, and acts respectively.

3. L. J. Savage, *The Foundations of Statistics* (New York: Wiley, 1954) (rev. ed., New York: Dover, 1972), chap. 2 and chap. 4, sec. 5.

4. By Robert Stalnaker, Allan Gibbard and William Harper, Howard Sobel and David Lewis. For developments by this group of philosophers, see Harper's "Sketch of Some Recent Developments in the Theory of Conditionals," Stalnaker's "Letter to David Lewis," and Gibbard and Harper's "Counterfactuals and Two Kinds of Expected Utility," all in *Ifs*, ed. W. L. Harper, R. Stalnaker, and G. Pearce (Dordrecht: Reidel, 1981); and Lewis's "Causal Decision Theory," in *Australasian Journal of Philosophy* 59 (1981): 5–30.

   The idea is not something that only a philosopher could love. Peter Fishburn in *Decision and Value Theory* (New York: Wiley, 1964) already suggests putting probabilities on conditionals: ". . . the probability that consequence o_j will result if strategy S_i is adopted by the decision maker or the probability that S_i will produce o_j." (p. 36). Stalnaker's suggestion (1972), made independently of Fishburn's work, focuses explicitly on the *subjunctive* conditional, and utilizes it for the analysis of Newcomb's paradox.

5. The figure is due to L. J. Savage commenting on the work of Jeffrey, in correspondence with Jeffrey. It is reported in R. C. Jeffrey, *The Logic of Decision* (New York: McGraw Hill, 1965).

6. Gibbard and Harper argue in "Counterfactuals and Two Kinds of Expected Utility" that Savage's system in *The Foundations of Statistics* can be interpreted as either evidential or causal decision theory, according to whether Savage's states are taken to be evidentially or causally independent of his acts. I believe that Savage intended the causal interpretation, although the book itself does not explicitly say so. The language of the following remark by Savage, in his "Difficulties in the Theory of Personal Probabilities" (*Philosophy of Science* 34 [1967]) is certainly suggestive of that interpretation: "Is it good, or even possible, to insist, as this preference theory does, on a usage in which acts are without *influence* on events . . . " (emphasis mine). There is also an internal reason to favor that interpretation. That is Savage's discussion in section 2.5 of the *Foundations of Statistics* of ways of generating an adequate set of states. The difficulty is that in an initial formulation of the decision problem,

the acts under consideration together with the states may not determine the consequences:

> The argument might be raised that the formal description that has been erected seems inadequate because a person may not know the consequences of the acts open to him in each state of the world. He may be so ignorant, for example, as not to be sure whether one rotten egg will spoil a six-egg omelet. But in that case, nothing could be simpler than to admit that there are four states of the world corresponding to the two states of the egg and the two conceivable answers to the culinary question as to whether one bad egg will spoil a six-egg omelet. It seems to me obvious that this solution works in the greatest generality, although a thoroughgoing analysis might not be trivial. [p. 15]

The general solution is, as I read it, to take the states of the world as consisting of descriptions of the preconditions of the decision adequate to determine the causal consequences of each act. This procedure gets us states which are *causally* independent of the act, but which may not be evidentially independent of the act. Newcomb's paradox is an example. Accordingly, I read Savage's theory as a version of causal decision theory.

7. Or, if we make the simplifying assumption that all value resides in the consequences,

Value $(A) = \Sigma_i DB(C_i \text{ given } A) \text{ Value}(C_i)$.

8. R. Stalnaker, "Letter to David Lewis," in *Ifs*.
9. The idea is taken seriously in R. A. Fisher, *Smoking* (London: Oliver & Boyd, 1959).
10. See R. Nozick, "Newcomb's Problem and Two Principles of Choice," in *Essays in Honor of Carl G. Hempel*, ed. N. Rescher (Dordrecht: Reidel, 1969).
11. This is explicitly done by Gibbard and Harper in section 12 of "Counterfactuals and Two Kinds of Expected Utility," in *Ifs*; and by David Lewis in "Prisoner's Dilemma Is a Newcomb Problem," *Philosophy and Public Affairs* 8 (1979): 235–40. See also the discussions of S. J. Brams, "Newcomb's Problem and Prisoner's Dilemma," *Journal of Conflict Resolution* 19 (1975); A. Rappoport, "A Comment on Brams' discussion of Newcomb's Paradox," *Journal of Conflict Resolution* 19(1975); and B. Grofman, "A Comment on 'Newcomb's Problem and the Prisoner's Dilemma'" mimeo, School of Social Sciences, University of California at Irvine (March 1977).
12. R. Stalnaker, "Letter to David Lewis," in *Ifs*.

13. A. Gibbard and W. Harper, "Counterfactuals and Two Kinds of Expected Utility," in *Ifs*.

14. D. K. Lewis, "Causal Decision Theory."

15. If we assume as Gibbard and Harper explicitly do, and as Savage also explicitly does, that ultimate value resides only in the consequences, this can be written as:

$$U_K(A) = \Sigma_i \text{ CHANCE}_{K, A} (C_i) \text{ UTILITY}(C_i)$$

If we think of $\text{CHANCE}_{K, A}$ as conditional chance of C on the condition A, $\text{CHANCE}_K(C \text{ given } A)$, we can rewrite the preceding as:

$$U_K(A) = \Sigma_i \text{ CHANCE}_K (C_i \text{ given } A) \text{ UTILITY}(C_i)$$

16. See n. 7 for more details on this reading of Savage. I think that this is the interpretation generally taken by statisticians and economists of unconditional expected utility models like that of Savage. Fishburn, in discussion of Savage, is quite explicit: "In this illustration it will be noted that the courses of action (or acts) have no effect on determining which state is the true state. Either the egg is rotten or it is not rotten, and nothing we can do will change this. In the statistical formulation this is always the case. That is, the true state among the states E_1, E_2, ... E_n is a factual matter and cannot be affected or altered by the contemplated strategies." (P. Fishburn, *Decision and Value Theory*, 51).

Similar statements can be found throughout the decision theoretic literature where an unconditional expectation is used. For example, see the comment at the bottom of p. 201 of F. J. Anscombe and R. J. Aumann, "A Definition of Subjective Probability," *Annals of Mathematical Statistics* 34 (1963): 199–205.

The idea of using an unconditional expectation to represent the causal considerations is explicitly raised in connection with the Newcomb problem by Isaac Levi in "Newcomb's Many Problems," *Theory and Decision* 6 (1975): 161–75. For reasons that I do not find convincing, Levi there *rejects* the causal paradigm.

17. Part IIC, B. Skyrms, *Causal Necessity* (New Haven and London: Yale University Press, 1980).

18. Because of the deterministic nature of the Newcomb example, essentially the foregoing analysis can be carried out in Savage's system.

19. E. Eells, "Causality, Utility, and Decision," *Synthese* 48 (1981): 295–329; and *Rational Decision and Causality* (Cambridge: Cambridge University Press, 1982.) Similar ideas are put forward in H. E. Kyburg, "Acts and Conditional Probabilities," *Theory and Decision* 12 (1980): 149–71.
20. R. Jeffrey, "The Logic of Decision Defended," *Synthese* 48 (1981): 473–92.
21. R. Jeffrey, *The Logic of Decision* 2nd ed. (Chicago: University of Chicago Press, 1983): 16.
22. In a more realistic model, deliberation is ended short of probability one. "There's many a slip 'twixt the cup and the lip." When we consider mixed or randomized strategies, slips are promoted from the status of accident to that of policy. We will return to this point later.
23. See R. Jeffrey, *The Logic of Decision*, chap. 11.
24. I discuss this more precisely in "On the Existence of Equilibrium Decisions" forthcoming.
25. B. Armendt, *Rational Decision Theory: The Foundations of Causal Decision Theory* Ph.D. thesis, University of Illinois at Chicago Circle, 1983. The key concept is conditional preference, preference for (A/H) is preference for A conditional on the hypothesis that H is true. In most cases one is indifferent between A and (A/A) but in Newcomb-type cases the hypothesis that A is true carries information about the state of the world that affects evaluation of A. In Armendt's analysis, an adequate partition of states of the world, $[K_i]$, must be such that this effect disappears for preference conditional on the state of the world, i.e. the agent is indifferent between (A/K) and (A/A & K).

CHAPTER 5

1. Quoted in B. Mates, *Stoic Logic* (Berkeley and Los Angeles: University of California Press, 1961), 43.
2. According to Mates, the Diodorian conditional is a material conditional universally quantified over time, and the Chrysippian conditional is true when the material conditional is logically true.
3. R. C. Stalnaker, "A Theory of Conditionals," in *Studies in Logical Theory* American Philosophical Quarterly Monograph (Oxford: Basil Blackwell), 98–112; reprinted in *Causation and Conditionals*, ed. Sosa (Oxford: Oxford University Press, 1965) and

in *Ifs*, ed. Harper et al. (Dordrecht: Reidel, 1981); and D. K. Lewis, *Counterfactuals* (Oxford: Oxford University Press: 1973).

4. E. Adams, "On the Logic of Conditionals" *Inquiry* 8 (1965): 166–97; Adams, "Probability and the Logic of Conditionals," in *Aspects of Inductive Logic*, ed. Hintikka and Suppes (North Holland Amsterdam,) (1966): 265–316; Adams, *The Logic of Conditionals* (Dordrecht: Reidel, 1975). Also see B. Ellis, "Epistemic Foundations of Logic," *Journal of Philosophical Logic* 5 (1976): 187–204; and R. Jeffrey, "If" (abstract), *Journal of Philosophy* 61 (1964): 702–703.

5. And goes some way toward answering the question posed by Allan Gibbard in "Two Recent Theories of Conditionals," in *Ifs*, 211–47.

6. B. Ellis, "Probability Logic" manuscript (1968).

7. R. Stalnaker, "Probability and Conditionals," *Philosophy of Science* 37 (1970): 64–80 (reprinted in *Ifs*).

8. D. K. Lewis, "Probabilities of Conditionals and Conditional Probabilities," *The Philosophical Review* 85 (1975): 287–315, (reprinted in *Ifs*).

9. This explains the phenomonae studied by Adams in his "Prior Probabilities and Counterfactual Conditionals," in *Foundations of Probability Theory, Statistical Inference, and Statistical Theories of Science*, ed. Harper and Hooker (Dordrecht: Reidel, 1976), 1–21, from the standpoint of the present theory. The priors in question will not always be *temporally* prior probabilities that the agent actually held in the past. They will be priors in that conditionalization will lead to the agent's current probabilities. I give a brief discussion of technical devices to deal with the recovery of priors in "Three Ways to Give a Probability Assignment a Memory," forthcoming in *Testing Scientific Theories, Minnesota Studies in the Philosophy of Science*, vol. 10, ed. J. Earman (Minneapolis, University of Minnesota Press).

10. To see the correctness of the informal description, notice that if one of our families of partitions is Omonotonic, then it follows that it has the property that if p entails q, then every member of Π_p is a superset of some member of Π_q consistent with p. each p-world (point in p) is in some member of Π_q consistent with p. Then by Omonotonicity, each p-world is in a member of Π_p which is a superset of a member of Π_q consistent with p. But every member of Π_p must contain a p-world, because our families always map a condition p onto a partition Π_p all of whose members are consistent with the partition.

11. Adams comes close to formulating the present theory for a fixed partition in his discussion of an *"ad hoc* two factor model" in his *The Logic of Conditionals*, sec. IV. 8.

12. H. P. Grice, "Logic and Conversation," The William James lectures delivered at Harvard University in 1967, some of which is in his "Logic and Conversation," in P. Cole and J. Morgan, eds., *Syntax and Semantics*, vol. 9 (Pragmatics) (New York: Academic Press, 1978).

13. In a talk given at the Pittsburgh Conditional Expected Utility Conference, November 1978, and in "Causal Decision Theory," *Australasian Journal of Philosophy* 59 (1981): 5–30.

14. I make this reduction, without much discussion in *Causal Necessity* (New Haven and London: Yale University Press, 1980), 138. David Lewis makes the same point with careful discussion of details in his "Causal Decision Theory." He there finds my informal description of the Ks as propositions about factors outside the agent's influence ambiguous between a broad and a narrow construal. Broadly taken, Ks could be about "a vast dispersed pattern of occurrences throughout the universe," narrowly taken "a 'factor' must be some sort of localized occurrence— event, state, emission, etc." I hope that it is clear here that what is required of the Ks is that they form a partition which captures *the decision maker's* beliefs about conditional chance. There is certainly no restriction to propositions about localized occurrences.

15. See my "Counterfactual Definiteness and Local Causation," *Philosophy of Science* 49 (1982): 43–50, for a discussion explicitly framed in terms of subjunctive conditionals.

CHAPTER 6

1. Cicero, *Tusculan Disputations*, bk. II, II.5.

2. Of course it might still be more convenient to talk about chances, but it is just that: *convenience*. No essential information or structure is lost if we eliminate statements of chance.

3. *Causal Necessity* (New Haven and London: Yale University Press, 1980).

4. E.g., see Hartry Field, *Science without Numbers* (Princeton: Princeton University Press, 1980). This has some relevance to our earlier example of metaphysics which is not *prima facie* eliminable. However, Field's representation still leaves us with propositions with metaphysical status of the general kind indicated.

5. This is discussed at greater length in my "Higher Order Degrees of Belief," in D. H. Mellor, ed., *Prospects for Pragmatism* (Cambridge: Cambridge University Press, 1980).

6. Although perhaps "metaphysical" in some other vague sense.

Index